POPE

# The Gospel of Mark

POPE FRANCIS

# The Gospel of Mark

*A Spiritual and Pastoral Reading*

Foreword by Ronald D. Witherup, PSS

**Maryknoll, New York 10545**

Founded in 1970, Orbis Books endeavors to publish works that enlighten the mind, nourish the spirit, and challenge the conscience. The publishing arm of the Maryknoll Fathers and Brothers, Orbis seeks to explore the global dimensions of the Christian faith and mission, to invite dialogue with diverse cultures and religious traditions, and to serve the cause of reconciliation and peace. The books published reflect the views of their authors and do not represent the official position of the Maryknoll Society. To learn more about Maryknoll and Orbis Books, please visit our website at www.maryknollsociety.org.

---



Published by Orbis Books, Box 302, Maryknoll, NY 10545-0302.



Edited and adapted from the original Italian publication: *Marco: Il Vangelo del segreto svelato* © 2017 by Libreria Editrice Vaticana, Città del Vaticano and Edizioni San Paolo s.r.l., Cinisello Balsamo (Milano).

The texts (homilies, meditations, speeches, Angelus, etc.) after the beginning of the pontificate are taken and adapted from: http://w2.vatican.va/content/vatican/en.html. The Italian sources are listed in the bibliography and were translated by Orbis Books.



Manufactured in the United States of America

---

Library of Congress Cataloging-in-Publication Data

Names: Francis, Pope, 1936- author.
Title: The gospel of Mark : a spiritual and pastoral reading / Pope Francis.
Description: Maryknoll, New York : Orbis Books, 2020. | "Edited and adapted from the original Italian publication: Marco: Il Vangelo del segreto svelato © 2017 by Libreria Editrice Vaticana, Città del Vaticano and Edizioni San Paolo s.r.l., Cinisello Balsamo (Milano)." | Includes bibliographical references. | Summary: "The Gospel of Mark is a pastoral commentary on the Gospel by Pope Francis, drawn from his homilies, writings, and speeches since he was elected pope"— Provided by publisher.
Identifiers: LCCN 2020011597 (print) | LCCN 2020011598 (ebook) | ISBN 9781626983908 (trade paperback) | ISBN 9781608338542 (ebook)
Subjects: LCSH: Bible. Mark—Commentaries.
Classification: LCC BS2585.53 .F74 2020 (print) | LCC BS2585.53 (ebook) | DDC 226.307—dc23
LC record available at https://lccn.loc.gov/2020011597
LC ebook record available at https://lccn.loc.gov/2020011598

# Contents

CONTENTS

# Foreword

*by Ronald D. Witherup, PSS*

Commentaries and studies on the Gospel of Mark, both technical and popular, abound. Mark has received much attention, in part, because it is the shortest of the canonical Gospels and because most scholars think it is likely the earliest of the four. Be that as it may, it is rare to find a coherent "reading" of Mark that is exclusively oriented to the spiritual and pastoral message of this rapid-fire story of Jesus of Nazareth. This book is one such resource.

Pope Francis is known for his lively interpretations of the scriptures. His homilies, allocutions, and published texts exhibit a profound love and respect for the scriptures as God's holy, living, and active Word. He makes no claims to be a biblical scholar, but it is evident that his reflections are always rooted in the biblical text. Here is a person who meditates deeply on the word of God and seeks to read it for its inherent faith perspective. Furthermore, his biblical interpretations are often pithy and to the point, filled with common wisdom and taking their cues from the colorful imagery that the Bible employs to communicate its divine message.

The present book on the Gospel of Mark is an outstanding example of the Holy Father's approach. As the introduction indicates, it is not a commentary on the whole Gospel, nor is it a full exposition of its theology. Rather, it is, as the subtitle indicates, a *spiritual* and *pastoral* reading of the Gospel from beginning to end, with contemporary insights offered along the way.

We should not be surprised at Francis's approach. Already in the first year of his pontificate, when he published the post-synodal apostolic exhortation *Evangelii Gaudium* (2013), he wrote about his particular interest in scripture in the context of giving advice about how to preach the word of God (nos. 135–159). His counsel is particularly pertinent to preachers of the Word but is also useful for anyone who reads the Gospels:

> First of all, we need to be sure that we understand the meaning of the *words* we read. I want to insist here on something which may seem obvious, but which is not always taken into account: the biblical text which we study is two or three thousand years old; its language is very different from that which we speak today. Even if we think we understand the words translated into our own language, this does not mean that we correctly understand what the sacred author wished to say. The different tools provided by literary analysis are well known: attention to words which are repeated or emphasized, recognition of the structure and specific movement of a text, consideration of the role played by the different characters, and so forth. But our own aim is not to understand every little detail of a text; our most important goal is to discover its principal message, the message which gives structure and unity to the text. (*EG* no. 147)

In this book, Francis puts his principles to work. Paying attention to the overall structure and the movement of the Gospel is exactly what he does in his treatment of Mark. He rightly focuses on the issue of Jesus's identity—often inaccurately referred to as the "messianic secret"—a major theme throughout the Gospel. The characters in Mark (including the disciples!) seemingly do not understand the nature of Jesus's *identity* as Son of God (1:1) and the suffering Son of Man (8:31–33; 9:31–32; 10:33–34). This is because they confuse his identity as the Messiah with a false understanding of what it means to be God's Anointed One. Jesus has not come as a victorious military leader to throw off the yoke of Roman tyranny. Rather, Jesus's true identity can be seen only at the foot of the cross. He came to serve and to give his life as a ransom for all (10:45; 14:24). It is no small irony that the one character in the story who gets this identity right is a Roman centurion (!) who, upon seeing the nature of Jesus's suffering and death on the cross, exclaims: "Truly, this man was the Son of God!" (15:39).

Another aspect of Francis's interpretation of Mark is that it is stamped with his Jesuit background. His reading of the gospel text is influenced by his long-term use of the *Spiritual Exercises of St. Ignatius of Loyola,* the founder of the Jesuits. This exquisite spiritual tradition invites Christians to enter more deeply into the mystery of our own Christian identity by following the life of Jesus of Nazareth carefully and finding ourselves within it. Many of the exercises, which are usually conducted during an intense thirty-day retreat, invite participants to use their *imagination* to enter into the life of Jesus. We become his companions "on the way." We participate in many incidents of his public ministry, and we join him in the passion, death, and resurrection. Although all four Gospels tell the same basic story, Mark's is the most compact and tightly organized; it is also recounted with great speed. Pope Francis's reading follows this outline from its inception to its conclusion, not line-by-line but section-by-section. Thus, there is constant movement back and forth between the biblical text and its impact in our lives. The Holy Father makes this transition seamlessly, with the result that we hardly notice when we have moved from hearing and seeing the story of Jesus to reflecting on its importance in our lives.

In short, this book shows Pope Francis as a master contemporary interpreter of the Gospel of Mark. Readers will likely want to digest each chapter slowly in order to get the full benefit of the pope's insights. Orbis Books is to be congratulated for making this English translation of the original Italian version available to a wider audience. It shows once more the capacity of Francis to inspire and educate the faithful with a down-to-earth, pastoral, and ultimately deeply spiritual message.

Ronald D. Witherup, PSS
Paris, March 4, 2020

*Sulpician Father Ronald D. Witherup, PSS, served as superior general of the Society of the Priests of Saint Sulpice from 2008 to 2020. A noted biblical scholar, he has authored many books and articles on biblical and theological themes, most recently* Galatians: Life in the New Creation: A Spiritual and Pastoral Commentary *(Paulist, 2020).*

# Introduction

## The Word Is Fulfilled Today

*by Gianfranco Venturi, SDB*

This volume dedicated to the Gospel of Mark follows the method already adopted in the Gospel of Matthew, the gospel of fulfillment. This latest volume collects the pope's homilies, reflections, and addresses on Mark's Gospel.

As with the aforementioned volume dedicated to the Gospel of Matthew, this book does not represent an exegetical systematic reading of the Gospel of Mark or a progressive *lectio divina* of passages from the Gospel itself; it is rather a collection of wide and various reflections-meditations of Pope Francis—a Jesuit, superior, pastor, bishop, and, today, pope—starting from sacred scripture. These written or oral fragments, taken from various sources, are arranged here following the order of the chapters in the Gospel of Mark. Together they provide the reader with the insights and reflections that Pope Francis proposes regarding these texts.

Consequently, we have a commentary with different tones, in which the Word shines as a light that illuminates personal, ecclesial, and social situations, and as an invitation to go out and "walk the courtyards, see the grasslands, take in the fragments but contemplate the forms,"[1] always as an echo of the voice of the divine teacher who today speaks to his people and to each individual—none excluded, believer or non-believer, good or bad—to announce the accomplishment of the Word in one's life and in the context in which one lives.

A number of authors have written that Mark's Gospel can to be considered the "Gospel of the catechumen" or, in other words, a Gospel that it is meant for those who are just beginning on the path of faith that will lead to meeting Jesus. A careful reading of the fragments gathered here—the words of Pope Francis, whether written or spoken—confirms what has been proposed by these authors. The fact is that a common thread in the Gospel of Mark is the identity of Jesus, which is summarized in the initial words: "The beginning of the good news of Jesus Christ, the Son of God." Therefore, this Gospel can be considered a guide in beginning a journey that progressively leads not only to knowing and re-knowing "Jesus Christ, the Son of God," but also to encountering him, not simply as a historical character but as a living person who is present to us today.

As you read and meditate on the Gospel of Mark and grow closer to Jesus, this book will help you discover the treasure hidden in the single lines or words of the Gospel, a treasure capable of making your heart burn today. Therefore, these pages are not intended so much for study, or even for preaching, but for those who want to be guided by Pope Francis, a master of prayerful silence, to enter into a simple and lively intimacy with the one who is the Word "full of grace and truth" (John 1:14), the Word made flesh as revealed to us in the Gospel, the "good news."

It will also be useful for those who accompany the catechumens in the rite of Christian initiation, to learn from Pope Francis how to read the Gospel of Mark so that it is not something far away, but a Word addressed to those who want to meet Jesus and relive his mystery today.

### *The identity of Jesus*

*Who is Jesus?* In his letter addressed to Eugene Scalfari, and to unbelievers, Pope Francis responds to this specific question: "The question that is repeatedly found in Mark's Gospel—*Who is this who…?*—is one that concerns the identity of Jesus, an identity that arises from an authority different from that of the world. It is an authority that doesn't exercise power over others. Instead it is one of service; it offers freedom and fullness of life, even to the point of putting one's own life at stake, experiencing incomprehension, betrayal, rejection, being sentenced to death, and being abandoned on the cross (Mark 15:39)." This summary of Francis's response is a thread that runs throughout the Gospel of Mark, outlining the identity of Jesus and culminating in his manifestation and the apparent total failure of his entire mission.

Mark's Gospel opens with simple and concise words: "The beginning of the Gospel of Jesus Christ, Son of God" (Mark 1:1). In their brevity, they outline two phases of the gospel narrative, each with a point of arrival; together they trace the path to knowing the true identity of Jesus. The two phases can be summarized as follows:

1. The hidden identity (1:1–8:30), which culminates in Peter's profession of faith: "You are the Christ" (8:29).

2. Jesus's identity revealed (8:31–15:39), which culminates in the amazed exclamation (profession of faith?) of a pagan, the Roman centurion, who had directed the whole crucifixion and was present at the death of Jesus: "Truly this man was the Son of God!" (15:39).

The healing of the blind man of Bethsaida (which has no parallel in the other Gospels) in combination with the transfiguration of Jesus on Mount Tabor can be considered a transition from the first to the second phase.

Throughout this journey Satan is at work, seeking until the very end to understand the identity of Jesus; this is what Pope Francis defines as "satanic curiosity."

### *The hidden identity (1:1—8:30)*

From the beginning of his preaching, Jesus maintained absolute silence on his messianic identity, and he imposed such silence on the three disciples who witnessed his transfiguration.

Only at the end, when he was about to begin his passion, did he break this silence. In response to the high priest, who during the trial asked him: "Are you the Christ, the Son of the Blessed?" Jesus replied, "Yes, I am" (14:61–62).

Scholars continually wonder why Jesus kept his messianic identity a secret. In speaking about the "messianic secret" they suggest that the term "messiah" evoked, for many of his contemporaries (including his disciples), the idea of a worldly messiah and that Jesus carefully avoided defining himself in this way. Certainly his gestures, miracles, and "talking of authority" led many to consider him as the awaited messiah, but Jesus always asked for silence to avoid any misunderstanding. Instead, he prepared people to welcome his true messianic identity, which would be different from all expectations, a real surprise, although in line with the scriptures, where "it was written" that he had to suffer, die, and then rise again.

The first part of the Gospel ends when Jesus directly asks the disciples the question: "But you, who do you say that I am?" Peter replies: "You are the Christ." From that moment, repeatedly, Jesus begins to teach several times that he has to suffer greatly, be rejected, killed, and rise again after three days—the revelation of his identity and his mission.

### *"Satanic curiosity"*

There were many who at the time (just like today) questioned the identity of Jesus, and the answers differed, as can be seen in the responses reported by the disciples. Even the devil persistently posed this question. "The devil," writes Pope Francis, "was intrigued by Jesus's personality, and feared God" (cf. Matt 8:31; Mark 1:34; 3:11–12). On many occasions, the devil tried to discover and confirm the identity of Jesus, to determine whether he was a child of God. "He searched in the desert," Pope Francis writes, "where he remained bewildered by Jesus's answer," and then "went away from him until the appointed time" (Luke 4:13). The Pharisees and Sadducees also set traps for Jesus, to see if, by answering with particular wisdom, he should reveal himself as the Messiah. Finally when Jesus was on the cross, the devil returned and stated, "If you are the son of God, . . ." knowing that, if he wasn't, the devil could claim victory (cf. 1:32–34; 15:29–32). Pope Francis calls all this interest on the part of the devil "Satanic curiosity," the curiosity proper to that "perverse generation," of Herod and Herodias (Mark 6:17), who, yesterday as today, go in search of signs and seek to test God. Jesus responds with silence (cf. Mark 15:5, 33, 34) and puts forward only the one true sign, that of Jonah (cf. Mark 8:12).

### *Jesus's identity revealed (8:31—15:39)*

After the second miracle, the multiplication of the loaves (cf. Mark 8:1–10), Jesus must ask: "Do you still not perceive or understand? Are your hearts hardened? Do you have eyes and fail to see? Do you have ears and fail to hear? And do you not remember?" (8:17, 18). In this same section of the Gospel of Mark, we are told of the healing of the blind man at Bethsaida (cf. Mark 8:8–26), the hometown of Peter and Andrew; the place, the situation, and what occurs are not purely accidental. Indeed, unlike all the other healings that happen instantly, here the blind man is led out of the town and, through a series of subsequent gestures on the part of Jesus, gradually begins to see: the blind man of Bethsaida symbolizes Peter and every disciple.

In other words, to grasp the truth about the identity of Jesus, the disciple must be willing to set off; the person must let himself or herself be led to the sidelines and agree to walk. "To answer the question that we all feel in our hearts: *Who is Jesus for us?*" writes Francis, "what we have learned or studied in catechism is important, but it is not enough." In order to truly know who Jesus is, "we must make the journey that Peter made" (8:27–33).

### *Jesus is the Christ, the Son of God*

After Peter recognizes Jesus as Messiah, Jesus helps the disciples understand what this means, but "the apostles," writes Francis, still do not understand the words with which Jesus announces the outcome of his mission through his glorious passion; they do not understand! Then Jesus makes the decision to offer Peter, James, and John a preview of his glory, the glory he will have after the resurrection, to confirm them in faith and encourage them to follow him on the way of trial, the way of the cross (cf. Mark 9:11).

From that moment of transfiguration—from the moment they hear the invitation from the voice in the cloud—the disciples are called to listen to, understand, and accept the logic of Jesus's Easter mystery. But despite repeated announcements, the disciples fail to understand, until Jesus is lifted up on the cross, where "in failure the secret of Jesus's identity and mission is revealed" (cf. Mark 8:35).

Pope Francis writes, "As Christ on the cross is growing weaker (the disciples flee, Peter denies him, people desert him, and he has no power to descend from the cross), the devil becomes more bold and powerful: 'It is your hour and the power of darkness' (Luke 22:53). The devil shows himself brazenly; he feels himself the winner. But the 'flesh' of Jesus is a hook with bait, a trap," says the Holy Father, "and the devil, raging, is overwhelmed by his own victory and takes the bait: that's when he swallows the hook and the *poison* that *kills* (cf. Mark 9:29–32)."

Faced with Jesus's total failure, with such an ignominious death, one feels displaced, because everything happened out of love—a love so great that only God is capable of it. Jesus thus reveals his divinity in this giving of his life for love. Pope Francis writes: "The centurion, who stood in front of him, having seen him expire, said: 'This man was truly the Son of God!' From then, like that pagan symbol of all unbelief, that pagan centurion who was at the foot of the cross carrying out orders, each of us must proclaim: 'This is the Son of God who saved me.' That's our part: sinner, pagan, and separated from Jesus—we proclaim: 'This is the Son of God!'" (Mark 15:39).

Satan is defeated by the cross, while Jesus is raised to victory on the cross: he is raised on the cross in the total gift of life and attracts everyone to himself. The women—the first fruits of all of us—who go to the tomb in the early morning on the "day after the Sabbath" carry spices for the anointing, but they are not spices having to do with death; rather, they are spices that signify *"participation in the glory on the cross"* (Mark 16:1).

### *The Gospel is Jesus Christ, the Son of God*

"The beginning of the Gospel of Jesus Christ, Son of God" (Mark 1:1). "With these words," notes Pope Francis, "the evangelist, Mark, begins his story," with the announcement of the good news that has to do with Jesus, but more importantly than being information about Jesus, *the* good news is Jesus himself. Indeed, reading the pages of Mark's Gospel, we learn that its title corresponds to its content and, above all else, that this content is the very person of Jesus. Jesus, his person, is the Gospel, is *the* good news. The reverse is also true: the *good news* is "Christ-Messiah, Son of God."

### *Memory of the wonders of God*

In his message for the Thirty-Second World Youth Day, Pope Francis recalls how Mary in the Gospel says: "Great things the Almighty has done for me." Those great things are not over, but they continue to be realized in the present. It's not about a distant past. Remembering the past does not mean being nostalgic or sticking to a certain person or period of history, but recognizing one's origins, always returning to what is essential and building what is new with creative loyalty. No one benefits from cultivating a crippling memory, or from always doing the same things in the same way. The Gospel holds the memory of what Jesus did and said. It is not inert remains; it is a source of new wonders of which God is the author.

### *The key to interpreting everything*

The Gospel is "Jesus Christ Son of God." This is the key that interprets life and history; it is "good news," which, however, as Pope Francis says, is always colored by the "bitterness of failure" (the paschal mystery; 1:1–2). Furthermore, this fundamental element finds its climax on the cross. There is no "good news" that does not include the mystery of the cross (8:31–33).

### *Event and Word for today*

As long as the Gospel is on a library shelf, it is a book like any other. But when a believer or a community takes it in hand, opens it, and reads it, it ceases being something dead, a story from another time, and it becomes event and Word, the first event-history that becomes Word. Yesterday's characters become today's characters—the disciples, the scribes and the Pharisees, the priests, Herod, and so on, but especially the poor, the sick, the hungry, the crowd, the sinners. We are also among these characters. We are also blind (10:46–52), paralyzed (2:1–12), unable to understand, eager for power (10:38–45). We too participate in gospel events, even those that seem to concern only Jesus, such as his baptism (1:9–11), or his being driven by the Spirit into the desert (1:12–13). We are partakers in these events: we are baptized in his baptism; we are tempted in the desert.

*New wine*

Commentaries are often written on certain passages or verses, and not without reason. Every time we read it, a Gospel passage takes on new meanings, gives rise to new reflections, opens up new ways to follow. The Gospel is always new, and it makes new those who receive it with an open heart. Consider, for example, the different reflections on the multiplication of the loaves (8:1–10) or the healing of the blind man in Jericho (10:46–52). "Our God," says Pope Francis, "is a God who always does new things. And he asks us to be open to new meaning. Jesus is clear on this, he is very clear: new wine in new wineskins. God must be received with openness, and this attitude of openness is called docility" (cf. 2:18–22).

***The Gospel that goes out***

The Gospel is not like a fence that closes us in or protects us from the cold or from contact with people. It is always moving outward, on the way from Galilee to Jerusalem, from Jerusalem to the "first Galilee" (6:14–29), and then from Galilee to the whole world.

From the very start, Jesus calls us to "be" with him. He calls us, not to be sedentary, but to walk with him (6:7–13). He invites us to cross the sea without fear of the storm (4:35–41) and to be brave in uncovering roofs so the paralytic can walk (2:1–12). The Gospel is not static. It involves ascending Tabor, a foretelling of the climb to Calvary. It lives and is always found in going out. The Gospel is "a divine thread that passes through human history and weaves together the history of salvation" (cf. 1:15).

When it seems that it's all over and has come to an end, "the Master always precedes us, walks ahead of us, sets us on our way, and teaches us not to stand still" (16:7).

### *A small seed*

"To bring his disciples and the crowds to an evangelical mentality and give them the right *glasses* to approach the logic of love that dies and rises, Jesus used parables, in which the kingdom of God was often compared to a seed that releases its vital force just when it dies in the earth. Resorting to images and metaphors to communicate the humble power of the kingdom does not reduce its importance and urgency, but gives the listener the space and freedom to welcome it and also refer it to himself" (cf. Mark 4:1–34). The seed of the Gospel is spread out over the earth. No one is excluded. The risk of sterility is overcome by the power of the Spirit. The Gospel, from a small seed, becomes large. Its growth is never the result of planning. Its growth is a process of continuity and discontinuity, always open to surprises.

### *Rejected and accepted*

Rejection of the Gospel leads to a people without memory, without prophecy, without hope. Such rejection creates a system that is closed, one that cages the spirit and enslaves the law (cf. 12:1–12). What is rejected and discarded becomes strong, the cornerstone. The story "that begins with a dream of love and appears to be a love story, then seems to result in a history of failures, ends with the great love of God who draws forth salvation out of the emptiness. His rejected Son saves us all."

### *Conclusion*

We can now recognize that the Gospel has its climax in the failure of Jesus on the cross. However, it is a failure which is the highest demonstration of a unique love, of which only God can be capable. For in that failure lies the resurrection, the glorification, like the seed placed in the ground that dies and hides nascent life.

The gospel story is not a beautiful story about an event in the past. When we read the story in faith, every event and every word are relevant today; we are all involved.

The catechumen who listens carefully to the Gospel feels that the words are addressed to him or herself. He or she is taking part in those events, and experiences new meaning in life through meeting Jesus. The seed sown in the field, sown in its old skin, becomes the new event, the new Word, the new life, eternal life.

*Translated from the original introduction by Gianfranco Venturi, SDB*

# 1
# The Beginning of the Public Life

## THE "GOOD NEWS" (1:1)[1]

***The key to interpreting life and history***

Life is not simply a bare succession of events, but a history, a story waiting to be told through the choice of an interpretative lens that can select and gather the most relevant data. In and of itself, reality has no one, clear meaning. Everything depends on the way we look at things, on the lens we use to view them. If we change that lens, reality itself appears different. So how can we begin to "read" reality through the right lens?

***The Gospel of Jesus, Son of God***

For Christians, that lens can only be the good news, beginning with the Good News par excellence: "the Gospel of Jesus Christ, Son of God" (Mark 1:1). With these words, the evangelist, Mark, begins his story not by relating "good news" about Jesus, but rather *the good news that is Jesus himself*. Indeed, in reading the pages of Mark's Gospel, we learn that its title corresponds to its content and, above all else, that this content is the very person of Jesus.

***The Easter mystery***

This good news—Jesus himself—is not good because it has nothing to do with suffering, but rather because suffering itself becomes part of a bigger picture. It is seen as an integral part of Jesus's love for the Father and for all humanity. In Christ, God has shown his solidarity with every human in every situation. He has told us that we are not alone, for we have a Father who is constantly mindful of his children. "Fear not, for I am with you" (Isa 43:5): these are the comforting words of a God who is immersed in the history of his people. In his beloved Son, the divine promise—"I am with you"—embraces all our weakness, even to dying and death. In Christ, even darkness and death become a point of encounter with Light and Life. Hope is born, a hope accessible to everyone, at the very crossroads where life meets the bitterness of failure. That hope does not disappoint, because God's love has been poured into our hearts (cf. Rom 5:5) and makes new life blossom, like a shoot that springs up from the fallen seed. Seen in this light, every new tragedy that occurs in the world's history can also become a setting for good news, inasmuch as love can find a way to draw near and to raise up sympathetic hearts, resolute faces, and hands ready to build anew.

## Jesus the Center and End of History (1:2–4)[2]

It is interesting that when the apostles proclaim Jesus Christ they never begin by saying, for example: "Jesus Christ is the Savior!" Rather, the apostles introduce their testimony by presenting "the history of the people." We see it in today's passage from the Acts of the Apostles (cf. 13:13–25). . . .

One cannot understand Jesus Christ apart from the history that prepares for him. Consequently, one cannot understand a Christian apart from the people of God, for a Christian is not a monad, someone who exists alone. No, he belongs to a people, to the Church, so much so that a Christian without the Church is an abstract idea, not a reality!

## The Baptism of Jesus (1:9–11)[3]

All four Gospels testify that Jesus, before taking up his ministry, wanted to be baptized by John the Baptist (Matt 3:13–17; Mark 1:9–11; Luke 3:21–22; John 1:29–34). This event gives decisive direction to Christ's entire mission. Indeed, he did not present himself to the world in the splendor of the temple; he could have done so. He did not announce himself with the sounding of trumpets; he could have done so. And he did not come vested like a judge; he could have done so. Instead, after thirty years of a hidden life in Nazareth, Jesus went to the River Jordan, together with many other people, and there waited in line with sinners. He wasn't ashamed; he was there with everyone, with sinners, to be baptized. Therefore, from the very beginning of his ministry, he manifested himself as the Messiah who takes upon himself the human condition, moved by solidarity and compassion. As he said in the synagogue of Nazareth when he identified with the prophecy of Isaiah: "The Spirit of the Lord is upon me, because he has anointed me to preach good news to the poor. He has sent me to proclaim release to the captives and recovery of sight to the blind, to set at liberty those who are oppressed, to proclaim the acceptable year of the Lord" (Luke 4:18–19). Everything that Jesus accomplished after his baptism was the realization of that initial design: to bring to all people the saving love of God. Jesus did not bring hatred, did not bring hostility; he brought us love! A love that saves!

He came close to the lowliest, communicating to them God's mercy that is forgiveness, joy, and new life. Jesus, the

Son sent by the Father, is truly the start of the time of mercy for all humanity! Those present on the banks of the Jordan did not immediately understand the full extent of Jesus's gesture. John the Baptist himself was stunned by his decision (cf. Matt 3:14). But not the Heavenly Father! He let his voice be heard from on high: "You are my beloved son, with you I am well pleased" (Mark 1:11). In this way, the Father confirmed the path that the Son had taken as Messiah, as the Holy Spirit descended upon him in the form of a dove. Thus, Jesus's heart beats, so to speak, in unison with the heart of the Father and of the Spirit, showing to all that salvation is the fruit of God's mercy.

We can contemplate even more clearly the great mystery of this love by directing our gaze to Jesus crucified. As the Innocent One is about to die for us sinners, he prays to the Father: "Father, forgive them; for they know not what they do" (Luke 23:34). It is on the cross that Jesus presents the sin of the world to the mercy of the Father: the sin of all people, my sins, your sins, everyone's sins. There, on the cross, he presents them to the Father. And with the sin of the world, all our sins are wiped away. Nothing and no one is left out of this sacrificial prayer of Jesus. Therefore, we must not be afraid of acknowledging and confessing ourselves as sinners. How many times have we said: "Well, this one is a sinner, he did this and that...," and judge someone else? And you? Everyone should ask oneself: "Yes, he is a sinner. And I?" We are all sinners, but we are all forgiven. We all have the opportunity to receive this forgiveness—the mercy of God. Therefore, we mustn't be afraid to acknowledge that we are sinners, to confess that we are sinners, because every sin was borne by the Son on the Cross. When we confess it, repenting and entrusting ourselves to him, we can be certain of forgiveness. The sacrament of reconciliation makes present to each one of us the power of forgiveness that flows from the cross and renews in our life the grace of mercy that Jesus purchased for us! We must not be afraid of our defects: we each have our own. The power of the love of the Crucified One knows no bounds and never runs dry. This mercy wipes away our defects.

We ask God for the grace to experience the power of the Gospel: the Gospel of mercy that transforms, that lets us enter the heart of God and makes us capable of forgiving and looking at the world with more goodness. If we accept the Gospel of the Crucified and Risen One, our whole life will be formed by his renewing love.

## We Are Consecrated by the Spirit (1:9–11)[4]

The word "Christian" means that we are consecrated like Jesus, in the same Spirit in which Jesus was immersed throughout his earthly existence. He is the "Christ," the Anointed One, the Consecrated One; we, the baptized, are "Christian," meaning consecrated, anointed. Therefore, dear parents, dear godfathers and godmothers, if you want your children to become true Christians, help them to grow up "immersed" in the Holy Spirit, that is, in the warmth of the love of God, in the light of his Word. Do not forget to invoke the Holy Spirit often, every day.

"Do you pray, Ma'am?"

"Yes."

"To whom do you pray?"

"I pray to God."

But "God" does not exist like this: God is person, and as person the Father, Son, and Holy Spirit exist.

"To whom do you pray?"

"The Father, the Son, the Holy Spirit."

We usually pray to Jesus. When we pray the "Our Father," we pray to the Father. But we do not often pray to the Holy Spirit. It is very important to pray to the Holy Spirit who teaches us how to raise the family, the children, so that these children may grow in the living presence of the Holy Trinity. It is precisely the Spirit who leads them forward. For this reason, do not forget to invoke the Holy Spirit often, every day. You can do so, for example, with this simple prayer: "Come, Holy Spirit, fill the hearts of your faithful and kindle in them the fire of your love." You can say this prayer for your children, and, of course, also for yourselves!

When you recite this prayer, you feel the maternal presence of the Virgin Mary. She teaches us to pray to the Holy Spirit, and to live in accordance with the Spirit, like Jesus.

## The Voice of the Father (1:10–11)[5]

Scripture and Tradition give us access to a knowledge of the Trinity, which is revealed with the features of a family. The family is the image of God, who is a communion of persons. At Christ's baptism, the Father's voice was heard, calling Jesus his beloved Son, and in this love we can recognize the Holy Spirit (cf. Mark 1:10–11).

## Driven by the Spirit (1:12–15)[6]

### *The trial and victory of Jesus*

The Gospel recalls the themes of temptation, conversion, and the Good News. Mark the Evangelist writes: "The Spirit immediately drove Jesus out into the wilderness. And he was in the wilderness forty days, tempted by Satan" (cf. Mark 1:12–13). Jesus goes into the desert to prepare himself for his mission in the world. He does not need conversion, but as a man, he must go through this trial both for himself, to obey the Father's will, and for us, to give us the grace to overcome temptation. Jesus's preparation consists in the battle against the evil spirit, that is, against the devil. For us too, Lent is a time of spiritual "contest," spiritual struggle: we are called to confront the Evil One through prayer in order to be able, with God's help, to overcome him in our daily life. We know that evil unfortunately is at work in our existence and around us, where there is violence, rejection of the other, building walls, war, injustice. All of these are the work of the Evil One, of evil.

Immediately following the temptations in the desert, Jesus begins to preach the Gospel, that is, the Good News, the second word. The first was "temptation," the second, "Good News." And this Good News demands our conversion—the third word—and faith. He proclaims: "The time is fulfilled, and the kingdom of God is at hand"; and then he cautions, "Repent and believe in the gospel" (v. 15), that is, believe in this Good News that the kingdom of God is at hand. In our lives, we always need to convert—every day! And the Church invites us to pray for this. In fact, we are never sufficiently oriented toward God, and we must continually direct our minds and our hearts toward him. To do this, we need to have the courage to reject all that takes us off course, the false values that deceive us by subtly flattering our ego. Furthermore, we must entrust ourselves to the Lord, to his goodness and to his project of love for each of us. Lent is a time of repentance, yes, but it is not a time of sorrow! It is a time of penance, but it is not a time of sadness, of mourning. It is a time of joyous and serious commitment to strip ourselves of our selfishness, of our "old self," and to renew ourselves according to the grace of our baptism.

## The Beginning of the Galilean Ministry (1:14–15)[7]

The Gospel today presents the beginning of Jesus's preaching ministry in Galilee. Saint Mark stresses that Jesus began to preach "after John [the Baptist] was arrested" (1:14). Precisely at the moment in which the prophetic voice of the Baptist, who proclaimed the coming of the kingdom of God, was silenced by Herod, Jesus begins to travel the roads of his land to bring to all, especially the poor, "the gospel of God" (v. 14). The proclamation of Jesus is like that of John, with the essential difference that Jesus no longer points to another who must come. Jesus is the fulfillment of the promises; He is the "good news" to believe in, to receive, and to communicate to all men and women of every time that they too may entrust their lives to him. Jesus Christ is the Word living and working in history: whoever hears and follows him may enter the kingdom of God.

Jesus is the fulfillment of divine promises, for he is the One who gives us the Holy Spirit, the "living water" that quenches our restless heart, thirsting for life, love, freedom, and peace—thirsting for God. How often do we feel or have we felt that thirst in our hearts! Jesus revealed it to the Samaritan woman, whom he met at Jacob's well and to whom he said: "Give me a drink" (John 4:7).

## Placing Jesus at the Center (1:14–20)[8]

The liturgical season that we just experienced centered on the wait for Jesus and then the coming of Jesus: his birth and the mysteries of his birth until his baptism. Thus, today begins a new liturgical season, and the Church shows us that Jesus is also at the center of this beginning. Indeed, the center of today's liturgy is Jesus: Jesus as the first and last word of the Father. In fact, God, who often and in different ways in ancient times spoke to our fathers through the prophets, recently, in these days, has spoken to us through the Son whom he established as heir of all things and through whom he also created the world: Jesus the Son, the Savior, the Lord: he is the Lord of the Universe.

It was a long journey to this moment of the manifestation of Jesus whom we celebrated in the Christmas season. But he continues to be the center of Christian life: Jesus Christ, Son of the Father, Savior of the world. There is no other; he is the One. And this is the center of our life: Jesus Christ, who manifests himself and shows himself, and we are invited to know him, to recognize him in life, in the many circumstances of life.

The point is to recognize Jesus, to know Jesus. And although it is good to know about the life of this or that saint or about the apparitions to that person here or there, one must never lose sight of the fact that the center is Jesus Christ; without Jesus Christ there are no saints. Of course, the saints are saints. They are great; they are important, but not all apparitions are true.

In this perspective, we should ask: Is the center of my life Jesus Christ? What is my relationship with Jesus Christ? At the start of the celebration of Mass, in the oration of the collect prayer, we asked for the grace to see, the grace to know what we have to do, and the grace to have the strength to do it. But the first thing we must do is look to Jesus Christ. There are three tasks, three things we can do to assure ourselves that Jesus is at the center of our life.

### *Know and recognize Jesus*

First, we need to know and recognize Jesus. At the beginning of his Gospel the apostle John says that many did not recognize Jesus: the doctors of the law, the high priests, the scribes, the Sadducees, some Pharisees. Furthermore, they persecuted him; they killed him. This makes clear that we must first know and recognize Jesus, discover who Jesus is. Does this interest me? It is a question that all of us must ask ourselves: Does it interest me to know Jesus, or am I perhaps more interested in soap operas or gossip or ambitions or knowing about other people's lives?

Indeed, to know Jesus, one must first be able to recognize him. And to know Jesus, there is prayer, there is the Holy Spirit, yes, but it is also a good practice to pick up the Gospel every day. . . . It is important to always take with you a copy of the Gospel, such as the pocket version, which is small and can be carried in a pocket or purse, so it is always with you. It is said that Saint Cecilia had the Gospel close to her heart: close, close! By keeping it always close at hand, you can read a passage of the Gospel every day. It is the only way to know Jesus—to know what he did, what he said.

Reading the story of Jesus is essential. The Gospel is the story of Jesus, the life of Jesus; it is Jesus himself. The Holy Spirit shows us that Jesus there. Please, do this: each day read a passage of the Gospel, a small one—for three, four, or five minutes. It is precisely in reading it that the Gospel is understood and works within us; it is the Holy Spirit who then does his work. This is the seed. It is the Holy Spirit who makes the seed sprout and grow.

### *Adore Jesus*

While the first task is to recognize and to know Jesus, the second task is to adore Jesus; he is God! It is important to adore Jesus. In the responsorial psalm we prayed: "Let us adore the Lord with the angels" (cf. Psalm 96). And if "the angels adore him" truly, then we should ask ourselves whether we adore him as well. Most often we pray to Jesus to ask or thank him for something, which is all well and good. However, the real question is whether we adore Jesus.

Let us consider the two ways of adoring Jesus. First, there is the prayer of silent adoration: "You are God; you are the Son of God; I adore you." This is "adoring Jesus." But then we must also remove from our heart the other things that we "adore"—those things that interest us more. There must be God alone. Other things are helpful only if they direct us to God; they are useful if they help us to adore God alone. Therefore, we must adore God, adore Jesus, and know Jesus through the Gospel.

There is a little prayer that we pray—"Glory be to the Father, and to the Son, and to the Holy Spirit..."—but we often say it mechanically, like parrots. Instead, this prayer is adoration, glory: I adore the Father, and the Son and the Holy Spirit. Adore, then, with little prayers. In silence before the grandeur of God, adore Jesus and say: "You are the only One, you are the beginning and the end, and I want to be with you for all my life, for all eternity. You are the only One." And in this way, banish the things that prevent you from adoring Jesus.

### *Follow Jesus*

The third task in order to have Jesus at the center of our life is what today's Gospel reading tells us: follow Jesus. When the Lord saw Simon and Andrew working—they were fishermen—he said to them, "Follow me." We must, therefore, follow Jesus, the things he taught us, the things we find each day when we read a section of the Gospel. And we must ask: "Lord, what do you want me to do? Show me the way."

In conclusion, it is essential always to keep Jesus at the center. This involves knowing and recognizing Jesus; adoring and following Jesus. Christian life is very simple, but we need the grace of the Holy Spirit so he may awaken in us this will to know, to adore, and to follow Jesus. For this very reason, we asked the Lord at the beginning in the collect prayer that we might know what we have to do and have the strength to do it. And, in the simplicity of every day—because to be Christians, the unusual, difficult, and superfluous things are not necessary—may the Lord give us the grace to know Jesus, to adore Jesus, and to follow Jesus.

## A Divine Thread (1:15)[9]

### *God is close*

A divine thread emerges, a thread that passes through human history and weaves together the history of salvation.... God is near, his kingdom is at hand (cf. Mark 1:15). The Lord does not want to be feared like a powerful and aloof sovereign. He does not want to remain on his throne in heaven or in history books, but rather he wants to come down and be among us in our everyday affairs, to walk with us. As we think of the gift of a millennium so filled with faith, we do well before all else to thank God for having walked with his people, having taken us by the hand, as a father takes the hand of his child, and accompanied us in so many situations. That is what we too, as members of the Church, are constantly called to do: to listen, to get involved, and to be neighbors, sharing in people's joys and struggles, so that the Gospel can spread ever more consistently and fruitfully, radiating goodness through the transparency of our lives.

### *God is real*

Finally, God is real. Everything about God's way of acting is real and concrete. Divine wisdom "is like a master worker" and one who "plays" in the world (cf. Prov 8:30). The Word becomes flesh, is born of a mother, is born under the law (cf. Gal 4:4), has friends, goes to a party. The eternal is communicated in spending time with people and through concrete situations. Your own history, shaped by the Gospel, the cross, and fidelity to the Church, has seen the contagious power of a genuine faith, passed down from family to family, from fathers to sons, and above all from mothers and grandmothers, whom we need so much to thank. In particular, you have been able to touch with your hand the real and provident tenderness of the Mother of all, whom I have come here [to Poland] as a pilgrim to venerate and whom we have acclaimed in the psalm as the "great pride of our nation" (Jud 15:9).

## The Invitation to Conversion (1:15)[10]

Jesus made conversion the first word of his preaching: "Repent and believe in the Gospel" (Mark 1:15). With this proclamation, he presents himself to the people, asking them to accept his word as God's final and definitive word to humanity (cf. Mark 12:1–11). With regard to the preaching of the prophets, Jesus insists even more on the interior dimension. In fact, conversion involves the whole person—heart and mind—to become a new creature, a new person. Change your heart and you will be renewed.

When Jesus calls one to conversion, he does not set himself up as a judge, but he calls from a position of closeness. Because he shares in the human condition, he therefore calls from the street, from the home, from the table.... Mercy toward those who needed to change their lives came about through his loving presence, involving each person in the history of salvation. Jesus persuaded people with his kindness, with his love, and with his way of being. He touched the depths of people's hearts, and they felt attracted by the love of God and were moved to change their lifestyle. For example, the conversion of Matthew (cf. Matt 9:9–13) and of Zacchaeus (cf. Luke 19:1–10) happened in exactly this manner, because they felt loved by Jesus and, through him, by the Father. True conversion happens when we accept the gift of grace, and a clear sign of its authenticity is when we become aware of the needs of our brothers and sisters and are ready to draw near to them.

How many times have we also felt a need to change that involves our entire person! How often do we say to ourselves:

"I need to change, I can't continue this way.... My life on this path will not bear fruit; it will be a useless life and I will not be happy." How often these thoughts come, how often! And Jesus, who is near us, extends his hand and says, "Come, come to me. I'll do the work: I'll change your heart. I'll change your life. I will make you happy."

Jesus who is with us invites us to change our lives. It is he, with the Holy Spirit, who sows in us this restlessness to change our life and be better. Let us follow, therefore, this invitation of the Lord and let us not resist, because only if we open ourselves to his mercy will we find true life and true joy. We have only to open wide the door and he will do the rest. He does everything, but we must open our heart so that he can heal us and enable us to go forward. I assure you that we will be much happier.

## Jesus Calls the First Disciples (1:17–18)[11]

In looking at your faces, the Mexican people have the right to discover [in their bishops] the signs of those "who have seen the Lord" (cf. John 20:25), of those who have been with God. This is essential. Do not waste time or energy, then, on secondary things, on gossip or intrigue, on conceited schemes of careerism, on empty plans for superiority, or on unproductive groups that seek their own interests. Do not allow yourselves to be dragged into gossip and slander. Foster in your priests a correct understanding of sacred ministry. For us ministers of God, it is enough to have the grace to "drink the cup of the Lord," the gift of protecting that portion of the heritage that has been entrusted to us, though we may be unskilled administrators. Let us allow the Father to assign the place he has prepared for us (cf. Matt 20:20–28). Can we really be concerned with affairs that are not the Father's? Away from the "Father's affairs" (Luke 2:48–49) we lose our identity and, through our own fault, empty his grace of meaning.

If our vision does not witness to having seen Jesus, then the words with which we recall him will be rhetorical and empty figures of speech. They may perhaps express the nostalgia of those who cannot forget the Lord, but who have become, in some sense, mere babbling orphans beside a tomb. Finally, they may be words that are incapable of preventing this world of ours from being abandoned and reduced to its own desperate power.

I think of the need to offer a maternal place of rest to young people. May your vision be capable of meeting theirs, loving them and understanding what they search for with that energy that inspired many like them to leave behind their boats and nets on the other side of the sea (cf. Mark 1:17–18), to leave the abuses of the banking sector so as to follow the Lord on the path of true wealth (cf. Matt 9:9).

I am concerned about those many persons who, seduced by the empty power of the world, praise illusions and embrace macabre symbols to commercialize death in exchange for wealth that, in the end, "moth and rust consume" and "thieves break in and steal" (Matt 6:19). I urge you not to underestimate the moral and antisocial challenge that the drug trade represents for the youth and for Mexican society as a whole, as well as for the Church.

## The Man with an Unclean Spirit (1:21–28)[12]

In the Gospel, it says that "they were astounded" (Mark 1:22). Why this "astonishment"? Because of the way in which Jesus taught. Furthermore, he taught them as one who has authority, and not as the scribes, that is, the doctors of the law. Indeed, all those people did teach, "but they did not enter the heart of the people" and therefore had no authority.

Authority is a recurring theme in the Gospel. In particular, we see this when Jesus finds himself "questioned, many times" by the doctors of the law, the Pharisees, the priests, and the scribes: "But by what authority do you do this? Tell us! You have no authority to do this! We have the authority." The essence of this question has to do with the difference between *formal authority and real authority*. While the scribes and Pharisees enjoyed "formal authority," Jesus had "real authority." But not because he was a seducer. In fact, if it is true that Jesus brought a "new teaching," it is also true that Jesus himself said he was teaching the law down to the last detail. The difference, compared to the doctors of law, lay in the fact that Jesus was teaching the truth, but with authority.

Thus, it is important to understand the nature of this authority. First, Jesus's authority was a humble authority. Jesus taught with humility. His authority was characterized by service, so much so that he advised his disciples to act in the same way: "Those who rule nations lord it over them, but it shall not be so among you. Let the greatest be the one who serves: he shall become the least, and he shall be the greatest" (cf. Matt 20:25–27). Jesus, therefore, served the people. He explained things so that the people could clearly understand. He was at the service of the people. He had the manner of a servant and this gave him authority.

In contrast, the doctors of the law "had the mindset of princes," and they thought: "We are the teachers, the princes, and we teach you. We do not serve; we command; you obey." Therefore, even if people listened to and respected them, they did not feel that the doctors of the law had authority over them. Jesus, however, never acted like a prince; he was always the servant of all, and this gave him authority.

A second characteristic of Jesus's authority was closeness. The Gospel states: "Jesus was close to the people, was among the people," and the people themselves "would not let him leave." The Lord was not allergic to the people. Touching lepers, the sick, did not disgust him. And his being close to the people gave him authority.

The comparison with the doctors, scribes, and priests is evident. They distance themselves from the people. In their hearts they despise those who are poor, those who are uneducated. They love to set themselves apart, walking in the squares, well dressed, in luxurious robes. They have a clerical mindset, and they teach with clerical authority. Jesus, instead, was very close to the people, and this gave him authority.

In this regard, we recall how close Blessed Paul VI was to the people. An example can be found in his apostolic exhortation *Evangelii Nuntiandi* (48), which recognizes the heart of the pastor who is close to his people. Therein lies the authority of that pope: closeness.

Jesus overturned everything, as if it were an iceberg. When we look at an iceberg we generally see its tip. Jesus instead overturned it, so that the people are at the top, and he who commands is below, and commands from below. Second, there is "closeness."

And last, there is a "third distinction" with respect to the doctors of law: "consistency." Jesus was consistent; he lived as he preached. There was a unity, a harmony, between what he thought, felt, and did—something that cannot be found in the attitude of the scribes and Pharisees. Their personality was split to the point that Jesus advised his disciples: "Do as they say, but not as they do." They would say one thing and do another. Jesus often described them as hypocrites. And one who feels like a prince, who has a "clericalist" attitude, who is a hypocrite, does not have authority. He will speak the truth, but without authority. Instead, Jesus, who is humble, who serves, who is close, who does not despise people, has authority. This, said the pontiff, is the kind of authority that the people of God can sense.

The authority that astonishes and wins over hearts is like that of the Good Samaritan, who is an "image of Jesus."

There's that man there: knocked down, beaten, left half dead in the middle of the street by bandits. And when the priest passes by, he goes around him because he sees blood and he thinks: "The law says that if I touch blood, I will be unclean.... No, no, I will leave." Later, when the Levite passes by, he probably thinks: "If I become involved in this, I will need to go to court tomorrow, to testify, and tomorrow I have many things to do. I must...no, no, no..." And so he goes away. Later, the Samaritan arrives. He is a sinner, from a different people. Unlike the others, has pity for this man, and he acts to take care of the man.

But in the parable, there is a fourth character: the innkeeper, who was astonished. He was astonished, not by the poor man's injuries, since he knew there were bandits on that path, on that road; and not by the behavior of the priest and the Levite, since he knew them and knew that this was their way of acting. The innkeeper was astonished by the Samaritan, since he did not understand why he would choose to stop and help. Perhaps the innkeeper thought: "This man is crazy! But he is also a foreigner. He is not Jewish; he is a sinner. But he is crazy. I do not understand!"

This was the astonishment—the same astonishment of the people before Jesus, because his authority was a humble authority, one of service. It was an authority close to the people and it was a consistent authority.

## Jesus Heals the Sick (1:29–34)[13]

The Gospels tell us often of Jesus's encounters with the sick and of his commitment to healing them. He presents himself publicly as one who fights against illness and who has come to heal humanity of every evil: evils of the spirit and evils of the body. The Gospel scene just referenced from the Gospel of Mark is truly moving. It says: "That evening, at sundown, they brought to him all who were sick or possessed with demons" (1:32).

When I think of today's great cities, I wonder: Where are the doors to which the sick are brought hoping to be healed? Jesus never held back from caring for them. He never passed by, never turned his face away. When a father or a mother or even just friends brought a sick person for him to touch and heal, he never let time be an issue; healing came before the law, even a law as sacred as that of resting on the Sabbath (cf. Mark 3:1–6). The doctors of the law reproached Jesus because he healed on the Sabbath; he did good work on the Sabbath. But the love of Jesus was in giving health, in doing good. This always takes priority!

## God Reaches Us through the Word (1:27, 45)[14]

God seeks to reach others through the preacher and displays his power through human words. Saint Paul speaks forcefully about the need to preach, since the Lord desires to reach other people by means of our word (cf. Rom 10:14–17). By his words Our Lord won over the hearts of the people. They came from all parts to hear him (cf. Mark 1:45); they were amazed at his teachings (cf. Mark 6:2), and they sensed that he spoke to them as one with authority (cf. Mark 1:27). By their words the apostles, whom Christ established "to be with him and to be sent out to preach" (Mark 3:14), brought all nations to the bosom of the Church (cf. Matt 16:15, 20).

## Jesus's Healing Signs (1:21–39)[15]

Today's gospel reading continues the narrative of Jesus's day in Capernaum. It was a Saturday, the Jewish weekly holy day (cf. Mark 1:21–39). Here, Mark highlights the relationship between Jesus's healing work and the awakening of faith in the people he meets. Indeed, with the healing signs that he performs, the Lord wants to arouse faith as a response.

Jesus's day in Capernaum begins with the healing of Peter's mother-in-law and ends with the scene of a crowd of townspeople who gathered outside the house where he was staying to bring all the sick people to him. Marked by physical suffering and by spiritual wretchedness of those who are sick, the crowd comprises, so to speak, "the living environment" in which Jesus's mission takes place. Jesus did not come to bring salvation in a laboratory; he does not preach from a laboratory, detached from people. He is in the midst of the crowd! In the midst of the people! Most of Jesus's public ministry took place on the streets, among the people: preaching the Gospel, healing physical and spiritual wounds. This crowd of which the Gospel often speaks is a humanity marked by suffering. It is to this poor humanity that Jesus's powerful, liberating, and renewing action is directed....

Miracles, in fact, are "signs" that encourage faith as a response, signs that are always accompanied by words that enlighten. Taken together, the signs and words arouse faith and conversion through the divine power of Christ's grace.

The conclusion of today's passage (vv. 35–39) indicates that Jesus's proclamation of the kingdom of God finds its most rightful place on the streets.... This was the journey of the Son of God and this will be the journey of his disciples. And it must be the journey of each Christian. The street, as the place for the Good News of the Gospel, places the mission of the Church under the sign of "going forth," of journeying under the sign of "movement" and never of idleness.

### Jesus Is Close in Times of Suffering (1:30–31)[16]

Jesus himself was born into a modest family that soon had to flee to a foreign land. He visits the home of Peter, whose mother-in-law is ill (cf. Mark 1:30–31), and he shows sympathy upon hearing of deaths in the homes of Jairus and Lazarus (cf. Mark 5:22–24, 35–43; John 11:1–44). He hears the desperate weeping of the widow of Nain for her dead son (cf. Luke 7:11–15), and he heeds the plea of the father of an epileptic child in a small country town (cf. Mark 9:17–27). He goes to the homes of tax collectors like Matthew and Zacchaeus (cf. Matt 9:9–13; Luke 19:1–10), and he speaks to sinners like the woman in the house of Simon the Pharisee (cf. Luke 7:36–50). Jesus knows the anxieties and tensions experienced by families and he weaves them into his parables: children who leave home to seek adventure (cf. Luke 15:11–32), or who prove troublesome (Matt 21:28–31) or fall prey to violence (Mark 12:1–9). He is also sensitive to the embarrassment caused by the lack of wine at a wedding feast (John 2:1–10), the failure of guests to come to a banquet (Matt 22:1–10), and the anxiety of a poor woman over the loss of a coin (Luke 15:8–10).

### Victory and Defeat (1:40–45)[17]

The passage taken from the First Book of Samuel (4:1–11) tells us that the people of God "are defeated in battle, in a war against the Philistines," while the Gospel of Mark (1:40–45) instead speaks about the victory over the disease of the leper who trusted in Jesus. Two opposite outcomes resulted from the protagonists' difference in faith.

### *The defeat of Israel*

The Israelites were defeated and everyone fled to his tent. There was a great slaughter: thirty thousand of Israel's foot soldiers fell. Thirty thousand! Furthermore, the ark of God was captured; and the two sons of Eli, Hophni and Phinehas, were slain. The people lost everything, even their dignity....

Why did this happen? The Lord was always with his people, so what led them to this defeat? The fact is that the people, step by step, had slowly distanced themselves from the Lord. They were living in a worldly manner and they even made idols for themselves. It is true that the Israelites went up to the sanctuary at Shiloh, but they did so as if it were a cultural custom: they had lost their filial relationship with God. Here, then, is the crux of the matter: they no longer worshiped God. Therefore, the Lord left them on their own. They had distanced themselves, and God left them to do as they pleased.

That is not all. After they lost the first battle, the elders asked: "Why has the Lord put us to rout today before the Philistines? Let us bring the ark of the covenant of the Lord." In that time of trouble, in other words, they remembered the Lord, but once again without true faith. Indeed, they went to get the ark of the covenant as if it were something—excuse me if I use the word—somewhat "magical." They said: "Let's bring the ark, it will save us! It will save us!" But in the ark was the law, the law that they did not observe and from which they had distanced themselves. In other words, there was no longer a personal relationship with the Lord. They had forgotten the God who had saved them.

Thus it happened that the Israelites brought the ark. The Philistines were afraid at first, but then they said: "We are men, let us go forth!" And they won. The slaughter was total: thirty thousand soldiers. Moreover, the ark of God was captured by the Philistines; the two sons of Eli, the delinquent priests who had exploited the people in the sanctuary at Shiloh, Hophni and Phinehas, were slain. It was a disaster. The people were left without soldiers, without young men, without God, and without priests. A total defeat!

*A lesson for everyone*

In the responsorial psalm (taken from Psalm 44[43]), we find the reaction of the people when they realized what had happened: "Lord, thou hast cast us off and abased us." The Psalmist prays: "Awake! Do not cast us off forever! Why dost thou hide thy face? Why dost thou forget our affliction and oppression?" This is the defeat: a people that distances itself from God ends up like this. It is a lesson that applies to everyone. Even today. We too, seemingly, are devout, we have a shrine, we have many things.... But is your heart with God? Do you know how to worship God? If you believe in God, but a somewhat nebulous, distant God, who does not enter your heart and whose commandments you do not obey, then this means that you are facing "defeat."

*The victory of the leper*

The Gospel, however, speaks of a victory. "A leper came to Jesus, and kneeling—precisely in this act of worship—said to him, 'If you will, you can make me clean.'"

The leper, in a certain sense, challenged the Lord, saying: "I am one defeated in life." Indeed, he was defeated, because he could not take part in common life; he was always "cast off," set aside. But he pressed on: "You can turn this defeat into victory!" Then, standing before this man, and moved with pity, Jesus stretched out his hand, touched him, and said to him, "I will; be clean." Thus another battle, but this one ended in victory within two minutes, while that of the Israelites lasted all day and ended in defeat. The difference lies in the fact that that man had something that spurred him to go to Jesus and pose that challenge. In other words, he had faith!

### *Faith is victory*

In the First Letter of John, it says: "This is the victory that overcomes the world, our faith." Faith always overcomes. Faith is victory. This is precisely what happened to the leper: "If you will, you can do it." The defeated ones described in the first reading instead prayed to God, brought the ark, but did not have faith; they had forgotten it.

When one asks with faith, as Jesus himself told us, it can move mountains. Recall the words of the Gospel: "Whatever you ask of the Father in my name, you will be given. Ask and it will be given you; knock and [the door] will be opened to you." Everything is possible, but only with faith. This is our victory.

### *Ask for faith*

Thus, let us ask the Lord that our prayers may always be rooted in faith. Let us ask for the grace of faith. Faith, indeed, is a gift and it is not learned from books. It is a gift to be asked of the Lord. "Give me faith." Indeed, "I believe, Lord," said the man who asked Jesus to heal his son: "I believe, Lord, help my feeble faith." We must therefore ask the Lord for the grace to pray with faith, so as to be sure, with the certainty that faith gives us, that everything we ask of him will be given us. This is our victory: our faith.

## Missionary Families (1:40–45)[18]

The work of handing on the faith to children, in the sense of facilitating its expression and growth, helps the whole family in its evangelizing mission. The faith then naturally begins to spread to others, even those outside of the family circle. Children who grow up in missionary families often become missionaries themselves. Growing up in warm and friendly families, they learn to relate to the world in this way, without giving up their faith or their convictions. We know that Jesus himself ate and drank with sinners (cf. Mark 2:16; Matt 11:19), conversed with a Samaritan woman (cf. John 4:7–26), received Nicodemus by night (cf. John 3:1–21), allowed his feet to be anointed by a prostitute (cf. Luke 7:36–50), and did not hesitate to lay his hands on those who were sick (cf. Mark 1:40–45; 7:33). The same was true of his apostles, who did not look down on others, or cluster together in small and elite groups, cut off from the life of their people. Although the authorities harassed them, they nonetheless enjoyed the favor "of all the people" (Acts 2:47; cf. 4:21, 33; 5:13).

2

# Healing and Preaching

## Jesus Heals the Paralytic (2:1–12)[1]

The Lord Jesus willed that the Church continue his saving work even with her own members, especially through the sacrament of reconciliation and the anointing of the sick, which can be united under the heading of "sacraments of healing." The sacrament of reconciliation is a sacrament of healing. When I go to confession, it is to be healed, to heal my soul, to heal my heart, and to be healed of some wrongdoing. The biblical icon that best expresses this deep bond of healing is the episode of the forgiving and healing of the paralytic, where the Lord Jesus is revealed as the physician of both souls and bodies (cf. Mark 2:1–12; Matt 9:1–8; Luke 5:17–26).

In fact, on the evening of Easter, the Lord appeared to the disciples who were locked in the upper room, and after addressing them with the greeting, "Peace be with you!" he breathed on them and said: "Receive the Holy Spirit. If you forgive the sins of any, they are forgiven" (John 20:21–23).

This passage reveals to us the most profound dynamic of this sacrament. The fact is that the forgiveness of our sins is not something we can give ourselves. I cannot say: "I forgive my sins." Forgiveness is asked for, is asked of another, and in confession we ask for forgiveness from Jesus. Forgiveness is not the fruit of our own efforts but rather a gift. It is a gift of the Holy Spirit who fills us from the wellspring of mercy and of grace that flows unceasingly from the open heart of the crucified and risen Christ. Second, it reminds us that we can truly be at peace only if we allow ourselves to be reconciled in the Lord Jesus, with the Father, and with our brothers and sisters. And we have all felt this in our hearts when we have gone to confession with a soul weighed down and with some sadness; and when we receive Jesus's forgiveness, we feel at peace, with that peace of soul that is so beautiful and that only Jesus can give, only him.

To receive the sacrament of reconciliation is to be wrapped in a warm embrace, the embrace of the Father's infinite mercy. Let us recall that beautiful parable of the son who left his home with the money from his inheritance. He wasted all the money and then, when he had nothing left, he decided to return home, not as a son but as a servant. His heart was filled with so much guilt and shame. The surprise came when he began to speak, to ask for forgiveness. His father did not let him speak; he embraced him, he kissed him, and he began to make merry. And I am telling you that each time we go to confession, God embraces us. God rejoices!

## A Seated Soul (2:1–12)[2]

The Gospel tells of the arrival of Jesus in Capernaum (2:12). So many people follow Jesus, always. Here there was no room for anyone, even around the door. One could think that those people followed Jesus for their own interests, to get something, perhaps health or a word of comfort. It could be that their *purity of intention was not complete; it wasn't exactly perfect. It's always mixed up, even in us.* Moreover, *how often do we too follow Jesus out of some interest, for some reason, or because it is convenient?* Indeed, purity of intention is a grace that is found along the way: the important thing is to follow Jesus, to walk behind Jesus.

Those people followed Jesus. They sought him because there was something in Jesus that attracted them to him: the authority with which he spoke, the things he said, and how he said them. Jesus made himself understood. He also healed people and many followed him, hoping to be healed. So many would do so that a few times he rebuked them when he realized that some of them were seeking him out for material interests. An example of this was the time when he said to the people, after the multiplication of the loaves: "But you are seeking me not to hear the word of God but because I have given you something to eat!" And he said this to illustrate the difference.

There were occasions on which people wanted to make Jesus king because they thought: "This is the perfect politician, and with him, things will go well; there will be no problems." But the people were wrong to think this way. Indeed, Jesus went away; he hid himself. But it is also true that Jesus always allowed people to follow him with this somewhat incomplete, imperfect purity of intention, because he knew that we are all sinners.

### *Watching from the sidelines*

In fact, the biggest problem was not those who followed Jesus, but those who remained motionless, those who stayed idle, on the sidelines, watching from their seats. In his Gospel, Mark writes: "Some of the scribes were sitting there. They were not following Jesus but were watching from the balcony; they were not walking along the path of life. They never took a risk; they only judged. They were the pure ones who did not want to get involved. And even their judgments were obstinate." Mark recounts that, seeing the crowd around Jesus, they were thinking in their hearts: "What ignorant people, what superstitious people!" How often, when we see the piety of simple people, does that clericalism which does so much harm to the Church come into play when we judge simple people by thinking of them as "superstitious"?

### *People without hope*

Of course, people are sinful. I am a sinner; we all are sinners. But people seek Jesus; they seek something; they seek salvation. Then there are those who, like the group of men on the balcony, sit there idle, watching and judging. And there are other "idle" people in life. Think of the paralytic man who had lain by the pool of Bethzatha in Jerusalem for thirty-eight years. He had nothing to do, was without hope, and was wallowing in his own bitterness (John 5:1–9). This man too was another idle one who did not follow Jesus and had no hope.

### *Taking risks*

Instead, the people who followed Jesus took risks. They took risks to meet Jesus, to find what they sought. Just think of the episode recounted in today's reading from the Gospel of Mark: "Unable to bring the paralytic to Jesus, because of the crowd, the people who accompanied him removed the roof above where Jesus was standing and, after they made an opening, they lowered the pallet." These men took a risk when they made the hole in the roof; they risked that the master of the house would sue them, take them to court, and make them pay. They took a risk, but they wanted to go to Jesus.

Let us recall also the story of the woman who had been suffering from blood loss (Mark 5:25–34). She took a risk when in secret she reached out to touch the hem of Jesus's garment. She risked public shame. She took a risk because she wanted her health; she wanted to get to Jesus. Let us also think of the Canaanite woman who risked being called a "dog," but she said to Jesus: "Yes, yes, but you can heal my daughter" (Matt 15:21–28).

Moreover, let us remember the sinful woman in the house of Simon. She entered, desperate, crying, her hair all disheveled, carrying perfume in her hand. And Simon looked at her and said to himself: "Shameless! If this man were a prophet he would know what sort of woman this is!" That woman, too, risked being judged. Like the Samaritan woman who took a risk when she began to question Jesus, this adulteress took a risk and found salvation.

These are all stories of women, in fact. That's probably because women take more risks than men. It is true. They are better, and we have to recognize this.

### *We are called to take risks*

Following Jesus is not easy, but it's wonderful. One always takes risks, and often one looks ridiculous. But you find something important: your sins are forgiven. This is because behind that grace that we ask for—good health, or the solution to a problem, or whatever—there is the desire to be healed in one's soul, to be forgiven.

We all know that we are sinners and that's why we follow Jesus, to encounter him. And we take a "risk" even in thinking: Do I take a risk or do I follow Jesus always according to the insurance company's rules? Up to this point, we have tried not to look ridiculous by not doing this or not doing that. But Jesus should not be followed "too politely." Indeed, by doing so, you remain seated, like the scribes in the Gospel who judged. Instead, following Jesus because we need something and also taking personal risks means following Jesus with faith: this is faith.

So we should place our trust in Jesus. We should trust him, with faith in his person. Consider again the men who made the hole in the roof in order to lower the paralytic's pallet down to Jesus, so that he could heal him.

In conclusion, make an examination of conscience by asking yourself some essential questions: Do I trust Jesus? Do I entrust my life to Jesus? Am I walking behind Jesus, even if I may seem ridiculous at times? Or am I sitting down, watching as others do, watching life? Am I sitting with a "seated" soul, so to speak, with a soul closed by bitterness, by a lack of hope?

## Open and Accessible (2:16)[3]

Jesus himself is the model of this method of evangelization that brings us to the very heart of his people. How good it is for us to contemplate the closeness he shows to everyone! If he speaks to someone, he looks into their eyes with deep love and concern: "Jesus, looking upon him, loved him" (Mark 10:21). We see how accessible he is as he draws near the blind man (cf. Mark 10:46–52) and eats and drinks with sinners (cf. Mark 2:16) without worrying about being thought a glutton and a drunkard himself (cf. Matt 11:19). We see his sensitivity in allowing a sinful woman to anoint his feet (cf. Luke 7:36–50) and in receiving Nicodemus by night (cf. John 3:1–15). Jesus's sacrifice on the cross is nothing else than the culmination of the way he lived his entire life. Moved by his example, we want to enter fully into the fabric of society, sharing the lives of all, listening to their concerns, helping them materially and spiritually in their needs, rejoicing with those who rejoice, weeping with those who weep. Arm in arm with others, we are committed to building a new world. But we do so not from a sense of obligation, not as a burdensome duty, but as the result of a personal decision that brings us joy and gives meaning to our lives.

## New Wineskins (2:18–22)[4]

A Christian who hides behind the notion that "this is how it's always been done..." is committing a sin, is idolatrous and disobedient, and is living a "half-hearted" life because his or her heart is closed to the newness of the Holy Spirit.

In the first reading, we heard that Saul, the king, was rejected by God for not obeying (1 Sam 15:16–23). The Lord told him that he would win in battle, in war, and that everything had to be utterly destroyed. But Saul did not obey.

Thus, when the prophet rebukes him for this and then in the name of God rejects him as king of Israel, he goes on to explain: "I have heard the voice of the people who took the best of this livestock to sacrifice to the Lord."

It is a good thing to sacrifice, but the Lord had ordered, had given a mandate to do something else. Thus Samuel says to Saul: "Has the Lord as great delight in burnt offerings and sacrifices, as in obedience to the voice of the Lord?" Obedience, therefore, goes further and surpasses even Saul's words of justification: "I listened to the people and the people told me: 'This is how it's always been done! The most valuable things go to the service of the Lord, either in the temple or as sacrifices. This is how it's always been done!'"

Then the king, who had to change his notion of "this is how it's always been done" says to Samuel: "I feared the people." Saul was afraid, and this is why he allowed what was contrary to the Lord's will.

### *The principle of life*

It is the same attitude that Jesus teaches in the Gospel (Mark 2:18–22), when the doctors of the law rebuke him because his disciples do not fast: "This is how it's always been done. Why don't your disciples fast?" Jesus responds with this principle of life: "No one sews a piece of unshrunk cloth on an old garment; if he does, the patch tears away from it, the new from the old, and a worse tear is made. And no one puts new wine into old wineskins; if he does, the wine will burst the skins, and the wine is lost, and so are the skins; so new wine is for fresh skins."

### *An open heart*

What does this mean? Has the law changed? No! It means, rather, that the law is at the service of humanity, that it is at the service of God, and for this reason we must have an open heart. The attitude of those who say, "This is how it's always been done," is born from a "closed heart." Instead, Jesus told us: "I will send the Holy Spirit and he will lead you to the full truth." Thus, if your heart is closed to the newness of the Holy Spirit, you will never reach the full truth. In addition, your Christian life will be a half-hearted life, a patched-up life, mended with new things on a structure that is not open to the Lord's voice: a closed heart, because you are not capable of changing the wineskins.

This was precisely the sin of Saul, the king, for which he was rejected. And it is also the sin of many Christians who hold onto what has always been done and do not allow the wineskins to be changed. They end up living a half-hearted, patched up, mended, meaningless life.

### *Listen to the voice of the Lord*

So, why does this happen? Why is it so serious? Why does the Lord reject Saul and then choose another king? The answer is given by Samuel, when he explains a closed heart, a heart that does not listen to the Lord's voice and that is not open to the newness of the Lord, to the Spirit who always surprises us. One who has such a heart, Samuel affirms, is a sinner. "For rebellion is as the sin of divination, and stubbornness is as iniquity and idolatry." Therefore, Christians who are obstinate, saying, "This is how it's always been done, this is the way, this is the path," are sinning: it is the sin of divination. It is as if they were to go to a palm reader. In the end, what has been said and what does not change—by me and my closed heart—becomes more important than the Word of the Lord. This is also the sin of idolatry: stubbornness. The Christian who insists, sins; it is the sin of idolatry.

### *What is the way?*

The question to ask with regard to this truth is: "What is the path?" The answer is found in opening our hearts to the Holy Spirit, discerning the will of God." It is true that always, after battles, the people traditionally took everything for sacrifices to the Lord and also for their own benefit, including gems for the temple. And it was customary, at the time of Jesus, for good Israelites to fast. However, there is another reality: there is the Holy Spirit who leads us to the full truth. And this is why we need open hearts, hearts that are not obstinate in the sin of idolizing themselves, that is, believing that what's most important is "what I think" and not "the surprise of the Holy Spirit."

### *New wine in new wineskins*

The message that the Church gives us today and which Jesus states so firmly is: "New wine in new wineskins!" Even traditional customs must be renewed in the newness of the Holy Spirit, in the surprises of God. The Lord gives us the grace of an open heart, of a heart open to the voice of the Holy Spirit, which can discern what must not change because it is fundamental from what has to change in order to be able to receive the newness of the Holy Spirit.

## The Sabbath (2:27, 3:6)[5]

On a day like today, a Sabbath, Jesus did two things that, as the Gospel tells us, precipitated the conspiracy to kill him. He was walking with his disciples through a field, a field of grain. The disciples were hungry and ate the heads of grain. Nothing is said to us about the "owner" of that field.... Underlying the account is the universal destination of goods. One thing is certain: faced with hunger, Jesus set the dignity of the children of God over a rigid, casuistic, and self-serving interpretation of the rules. When the doctors of the law complained with hypocritical indignation, Jesus reminded them that God desires love, not sacrifice, and explained to them that the Sabbath was made for human beings and not human beings for the Sabbath (cf. Mark 2:27). He confronted their hypocritical and smug thinking with the humble understanding of the heart,[6] which always puts people first and refuses to allow particular mindsets to obstruct its freedom to live, love, and serve our neighbor.

And then that same day, Jesus did something "worse," something that irritated even more the hypocrites and those filled with pride who were watching him, looking for some excuse to trap him. He cured a man's withered hand: a hand, that powerful symbol of work, of labor. Jesus restored the man's ability to work, and thereby restored his dignity. How many withered hands are there, how many persons deprived of the dignity of work, because the hypocrites, in order to defend unjust systems, are opposed to their being healed? Sometimes I think that when you, the organized poor, create your own work—establishing a cooperative, restoring a ruined factory, recycling the refuse of the consumer society, braving the elements in order to sell your wares in a public square, reclaiming a parcel of farm land to feed the hungry—whenever you do these things, you are imitating Jesus, because you are trying to heal, even if minimally and provisionally, the atrophy of the dominant socioeconomic system, which is unemployment. I am not surprised that at times you find yourselves being watched or persecuted, nor am I surprised that the proud have no interest in what you are saying.

On that Sabbath day, Jesus put his life on the line, because after he had healed the man's hand, the Pharisees and the Herodians (Mark 3:6), two rival parties that feared the people and the Roman Empire, began to scheme and plot to kill him. I know that many of you lay your own lives on the line. I know—and I want to say this—that there are some who are not here today because they did lay down their lives.... But there is no greater love than to give one's life. That is what Jesus teaches us.

3

# The Teaching of Jesus

## Healing and the Law (3:1–6)[1]

Jesus sends his disciples to perform the same work he does. He gives them the power to heal, to draw close to the sick and to heal their deepest wounds (cf. Matt 10:1). We must keep in mind what he says to the disciples in the scene of the man born blind (cf. John 9:1–5). The disciples, with the blind man there in front of them, argue about who sinned—this man or his parents—that he was born blind. The Lord says clearly that neither the man nor his parents sinned; the man is blind in order that the works of God might be made manifest in him. And Jesus heals him. This is the glory of God! This is the Church's task! To help the sick, not to get lost in gossip; to always help, comfort, relieve, be close to the sick: this is the task.

### *Constant prayer*

The Church invites us to pray constantly for her own loved ones stricken with suffering. We must never cease praying for the sick. Instead, we must pray more, both personally and as a community. Consider the gospel scene of the Canaanite woman (cf.

Matt 15:21–28). She is a pagan woman. She is not of the people of Israel, but a pagan who implores Jesus to heal her daughter. To test her faith, Jesus at first responds harshly: "I cannot. I must think first of the sheep of Israel." The woman does not give up—when a mother asks for help for her infant, she never gives up; we all know that mothers fight for their children—and she replies: "Even dogs are given something when their masters have eaten," as if to say: "At least treat me like a dog!" Jesus then says to her: "Woman, great is your faith! Be it done for you as you desire" (v. 28).

***Human illness***

In the face of illness, even in families, difficulties arise due to human weakness. But in general, times of illness help family bonds grow stronger. How important it is to teach children, starting from childhood, about solidarity in times of illness. An education that protects against sensitivity for human illness withers the heart. It allows young people to be "anesthetized" against the suffering of others, incapable of facing suffering and of living the experience of limitation. How often do we see a man or woman arrive at work with a weary face, with a tired countenance, and, when we ask them, "What happened?" they answer: "I slept only two hours because we are taking turns at home to be close to our boy, our girl, our sick one, our grandfather, our grandmother." And the day of work goes on. These are heroic deeds, the heroism of families—that hidden heroism carried out with tenderness and courage when someone at home is sick.

The weakness and suffering of our dearest and most cherished loved ones can be, for our children and grandchildren, a school of life. It's important to teach our children and our grandchildren to understand this closeness in illness at home—a closeness that grows when times of illness are accompanied by prayer and the affectionate and thoughtful actions of relatives. The Christian community really knows that the family, in the trial of illness, should not be left on its own. We must say "thank you" to the Lord for those beautiful experiences of ecclesial fraternity that help families get through the difficult moments of pain and suffering. This Christian closeness, expressed in loving actions from family to family, is a real treasure for the parish. It is a treasure of wisdom that helps families in difficult moments to understand the kingdom of God better than many discourses! Those actions are God's caresses.

## The Daily Struggle (3:7–12)[2]

The gospel passage makes repeated references to a "multitude": a great multitude from all over followed Jesus. The people in this crowd were throwing themselves at him, to touch him. It was a crowd that "came to him in great numbers from Judea, Jerusalem, Idumea, beyond the Jordan, and the region around Tyre and Sidon." One might ask: Why did this multitude come? Why this enthusiasm? What did they need?

The Gospel itself tells us that there were sick people who were seeking to be healed but there were also many people who came to listen to him. Indeed, these people liked hearing Jesus, because he did not speak like their leaders, but instead with authority. Certainly, it was a multitude of people who came spontaneously: they weren't brought on buses, as we have seen so often when protests are organized and many have to go "to prove" they were present and so not lose their jobs.

These people went because they felt something. And they were so numerous that Jesus had to ask for a boat and move out from the shore so that the crowd would not crush him. But what was their real motive? In the Gospel, Jesus himself explains this sort of social phenomenon. He says: "No one can come to me unless drawn by the Father" (John 6:44). In fact, whether this crowd went to Jesus out of "need" or because "some were curious," the true reason is seen in the fact that the crowd had been drawn by the Father: it was the Father who drew the crowd to Jesus. And Christ was not indifferent, like a detached teacher who spoke his words and then washed his hands. No! This crowd touched Jesus's heart. We read in the Gospel that "he had compassion for them, because they were harassed and helpless, like sheep without a shepherd" (Matt 9:36).

Therefore, the Father, through the Holy Spirit, draws people to Jesus. It is useless to look for all the reasons. Every reason can be considered possible, but it is not enough to make one finger move. You cannot move or take a step with only abstract reasoning. What is truly necessary and decisive, however, is that the Father draws you to Jesus.

### *The struggle*

It is curious that while this passage speaks about Jesus, of the crowd and their enthusiasm, and of the love with which Jesus received and healed them, there is also something extraordinary. It is written: "Whenever the unclean spirits beheld him, they fell down before him and cried out, 'You are the Son of God!'"

This is precisely the truth; this is the reality that every one of us feels when we approach Jesus and what the impure spirits try to impede; they wage war on us.

Someone might object: "Father, I am very Catholic; I always go to Mass. . . . But I never have these temptations, thank God!"

Yet it isn't so. The response is: "No! Pray, since you are on the wrong path!"—because a Christian life without temptations is not Christian: it is ideological, it is gnostic, but it is not Christian. In fact, it happens that when the Father draws people to Jesus, there is another who draws in the opposite direction and wages war within you. Thus Saint Paul speaks of the Christian life as a struggle: a struggle every day to win, to destroy Satan's empire, the empire of evil. This is the reason Jesus came, to destroy Satan! To destroy his influence on our hearts.

It seems that in this passage both Jesus and the crowd seem to disappear, leaving only the Father and the impure spirit—the spirit of evil. The Father who draws the people to Jesus and the evil spirit who tries to destroy, always!

Christian life is a struggle in which either you can let yourself be drawn to Jesus, through the Father, or you can say, "I'm tranquil, at peace" . . . but in the hands of this multitude, of these impure spirits. However, if you want to go forward, you must fight! You must allow yourself to feel your heart struggling, so that Jesus may win.

Therefore, all Christians must make an examination of conscience and ask themselves: Do I feel this struggle in my heart? Do I feel this conflict between comfort or service to others, between having a little fun or praying and adoring the Father, between one thing and the other? Do I feel the will to do good or is there something that stops me? And finally, do I believe that my life moves Jesus's heart? If I don't believe this then I must pray to believe it, so that he may grant me this grace.

## The Twelve Pillars (3:13–19)[3]

There is a word in this passage of the Gospel that draws our attention: Jesus "appointed." This word appears twice. Mark writes: "He appointed twelve, whom he also named apostles." And then he repeats: "He appointed the twelve," and he named them, one after another. Hence, from among all the people who followed him, Jesus called those whom he wanted. In other words, there is a choice: Jesus chose those he wanted. And, of course, he appointed the twelve, whom we call apostles.

Indeed, there were others: there were disciples, and on one occasion the Gospel speaks of seventy-two. But they were something else.

The twelve were appointed to be with him, and to be sent out to proclaim the message with the authority to cast out demons. It is the most important group that Jesus chose, so "that they might be with him," closer, and that "he might send them forth to preach" the Gospel and "to have the authority to drive out demons," Mark adds. These twelve were the very first bishops, the first group of bishops.

The twelve "elected ones" were conscious of the importance of their election. After Jesus ascended into heaven, Peter spoke to the others and explained to them that, in light of Judas's betrayal, something had to be done. Thus, those who had been with Jesus from the baptism of John until the ascension chose someone to witness with them—as Peter says—to the resurrection. This is how Judas's place was filled. It was taken by Matthias. Matthias was elected.

The liturgy of the Church, referring to certain expressions of Paul, calls the twelve "the pillars of the Church." Yes, the apostles are the pillars of the Church. And the bishops are the pillars of the Church. The election of Matthias was the Church's first episcopal ordination.

Today, I would like to say a few words about bishops. We bishops have the responsibility of being witnesses: witnesses that the Lord Jesus lives, that the Lord Jesus is risen, that the Lord Jesus walks with us, that the Lord Jesus saves us, that the Lord Jesus gave his life for us, that the Lord Jesus is our hope, and that the Lord Jesus always welcomes us and forgives us. This is the witness. Therefore, our life must be a witness, a true witness to the resurrection of Christ.

When Jesus, as Mark tells us, makes this choice of the twelve, he has two reasons. The first reason is so that they might be with him. This is why the bishop is obliged to be with Jesus.

Indeed, it is a bishop's first duty: to be with Jesus. The second reason has to do with the fact that in the early days, when the problem arose that the orphans and widows were not being well looked after, the bishops—these twelve—gathered and pondered what to do. And they decided to introduce the figure of the deacon, saying: "Let the deacons look after the orphans and the widows." Meanwhile, Peter says, the twelve have two tasks: praying and proclaiming the Gospel.

### *Prayer and witness*

The bishop's first task is to be with Jesus in prayer. Indeed, the bishop's first task is not making pastoral plans... no, no! It is praying. This is the first task. The second task is being a witness, that is, preaching: preaching the salvation that the Lord Jesus brought us.

The two tasks are not easy, but it is precisely these two tasks that strengthen the pillars of the Church. In fact, should these pillars weaken because the bishop doesn't pray or he prays very little, or he forgets to pray; or because the bishop does not proclaim the Gospel, occupying himself instead with other things, the Church weakens; she suffers. The people of God suffer. This happens because the pillars are weak.

This is why I would like to encourage you today to pray for us bishops because we too are sinners, we too have weaknesses, and we too run the risk faced by Judas: he too was chosen as a pillar. And we too run the risk of not praying, of doing something other than proclaiming the Gospel and driving out demons. I invite you to pray that the bishops might be what Jesus wanted and that we all might bear witness to the resurrection of Jesus.

After all, the people of God pray for the bishops. During every Mass we pray for the bishops. We pray for Peter, the head of the episcopal college, and we pray for the local bishop. But this may not suffice, for we say the name out of habit and move on. It is important to pray for the bishop from the heart, to ask the Lord: "Lord, take care of my bishop; take care of all the bishops, and send us bishops who are true witnesses, bishops who pray and bishops who help us, through their preaching, to understand the Gospel, to be certain that you, Lord, are living, you are among us" . . .

Therefore, we are all obliged to pray for our bishops, but it is a duty of love, the duty of children to the Father, the duty of brothers and sisters, that the family may remain united in the confession of Jesus Christ, living and risen.

## Trust in Preaching (3:14)[4]

Let us renew our confidence in preaching, based on the conviction that it is God who seeks to reach out to others through the preacher, and that he displays his power through human words. Saint Paul speaks forcefully about the need to preach, since the Lord desires to reach other people by means of our word (cf. Rom 10:14–17). By his words, our Lord won over the hearts of the people; they came from everywhere to hear him (cf. Mark 1:45); they were amazed at his teachings (cf. Mark 6:2), and they sensed that he spoke to them as one with authority (cf. Mark 1:27). By their words, the apostles, whom Christ established "to be with him and to be sent out to preach" (Mark 3:14), brought all nations to the bosom of the Church (cf. Matt 16:15, 20).

## Hearts Re-created (3:17)[5]

The Lord never tires of forgiving us. Indeed, he renews the wineskins in which we receive that forgiveness. For the new wine of his mercy he uses a new wineskin, not one that is patched or old. That wineskin is mercy itself: his own mercy, which we experience and then show in helping others.

A heart that has known mercy is not old and patched, but new and re-created. It is the heart for which David prayed: "A pure heart create for me, O God, put a steadfast spirit within me" (Ps 50:12). That heart, created anew, is a good vessel; it is no longer battered and leaky. The liturgy echoes the heartfelt conviction of the Church in the beautiful prayer: "O God who wonderfully created the universe, then more wonderfully re-created it in the redemption" (first reading of the Easter Vigil).

The best practitioners of the mercy that rights wrongs are those who know that they themselves have been shown mercy with regard to the same evil. Look at yourself and think of your own story; remind yourself of your story and you will discover so much mercy! We see this in the case of addiction counselors: those who have overcome their own addiction are usually those who can best understand, help, and challenge others. So too, the best confessors are usually themselves good penitents.... Augustine was healed in his regret for being a latecomer. This troubled him and in his yearning to make up for lost time he was healed: "Late have I loved thee." He would find a creative and loving way to compensate by writing his *Confessions*.

## Familiarity with God (3:31–35)[6]

A pastor serenely yet passionately proclaims the word of God. He encourages believers to aim high. He will enable his brothers and sisters to hear and experience God's promise, which can expand their experience of motherhood and fatherhood within the horizon of a new "familiarity" with God (cf. Mark 3:31–35).

A pastor watches over the dreams, the lives, and the growth of his flock. This "watchfulness" is the result not of talking but of shepherding. Only one capable of standing in the midst of the flock can be watchful, not someone who is afraid of questions, afraid of contact and accompaniment. A pastor keeps watch first and foremost with prayer, supporting the faith of his people and instilling confidence in the Lord, in his presence. A pastor remains vigilant by helping people to lift their gaze in times of discouragement, frustration, and failure.

## The Food of Jesus (3:34–35)[7]

At the beginning of the celebration, we asked the Lord: "Guide us to act according to your will, so that we may bear the fruit of good works."

When Jesus came into the world, he said, "Sacrifices and offerings you have not desired" (Heb 10:5), because they are temporary; not useless, but temporary. He continued, "A body you have prepared for me; in burnt offerings and sin offerings you have taken no pleasure. Then I said, 'See, God, I have come to do your will, O God'" (Heb 10:5–7). This act of Christ, of coming into the world to do the will of God, is what absolves us. He is the sacrifice, the true sacrifice that, once and for all time, has absolved us.

Jesus comes to do God's will and begins in a powerful manner, just as he ends his life, on the cross. Indeed, he began his earthly journey by "humbling himself," as Paul writes to the Philippians: He "emptied himself, taking the form of a slave . . . and became obedient to the point of death—even death on a cross" (2:7–8). Consequently, obedience to God's will is the way of Jesus, who says: "I come to do the will of God." It is also the path of holiness of the Christian, for it was the very path of our absolution: that God's plan be realized, and that the salvation of God be accomplished. It is the opposite of what happened in the earthly paradise, with Adam's disobedience. It was that disobedience that brought evil to all humanity.

In essence, sins are acts of not obeying God, of not doing God's will. However, the Lord teaches us that this is the path, there is no other. It is a path that begins with Jesus: in heaven, in the will of obeying the Father, and on earth, it begins with Our Lady, at the moment in which she says to the angel: "Let it be with me according to your word" (Luke 1:38). And with that "yes" to God, the Lord began his journey among us.

It is important for Jesus to do the will of God. This is evidenced in the encounter with the Samaritan woman, when in that southern region, in the heat of the desert, the disciples said to him: "Rabbi, eat something." But he answered: "My food is to do the will of him who sent me and to complete his work" (cf. John 4:31–34). In this manner, he made them understand that for him, God's will was like food that gave him strength that enabled him to go on. He later explained to the disciples: "I have come down from heaven, not to do my own will, but to do the will of him who sent me" (cf. John 6:38).

This is the food of Jesus, and it is also the Christian path. He has shown us the example for our life. It is not easy to do the will of God because every day so many options are presented to us on a platter: Do this, it's good; it's not bad. Instead, we should ask ourselves: Is it God's will? How am I doing in fulfilling God's will? First, ask for grace, pray and ask for the grace of the desire to do God's will. This is a grace.

Next, we must ask ourselves: Do I pray that the Lord may give me the desire to do his will? Or do I look for compromises, because I'm afraid of God's will? Additionally, we must pray to know God's will for us and for our lives, the decisions that we have to make now, how we are to manage things. It is thus, a prayer to *want to do* God's will and a prayer to *know* God's will. And once I know God's will, then there is a third prayer: to *fulfill* it. To fulfill that will, which is not mine but his.

Lord, give all of us the grace that one day your Son may say of us what he said of the group who in this passage from

Mark were seated around him: "Here are my mother and my brothers! Whoever does the will of God is my brother and sister and mother" (Mark 3:34–35). By doing God's will, we become part of Jesus's family. It makes us mother, father, sister, brother to Jesus. May the Lord give us the grace of this familiarity with him, a familiarity that really means doing God's will.

4

# The Parables of Jesus

### THE SEED OF THE KINGDOM (4:1–39)[1]

To introduce his disciples and the crowds to the gospel mindset and to give them the right "lens" needed to see and embrace the love that dies and rises, Jesus uses parables. He frequently compares the kingdom of God to a seed that releases its potential for life precisely when it falls to the earth and dies (cf. Mark 4:1–34). This use of images and metaphors to convey the quiet power of the kingdom does not detract from its importance and urgency; rather, it is a merciful way of making space for the listener to accept and appropriate that power freely. It is also a most effective way to express the immense dignity of the paschal mystery, leaving it to images, rather than concepts, to communicate the paradoxical beauty of new life in Christ. In that life, hardship and the cross do not obstruct, but rather bring about God's salvation. Weakness proves stronger than any human power, and failure can be the prelude to the fulfillment of all things in love. This is how hope in the kingdom of God matures and deepens: it is "as if someone would scatter seed on the ground, and would sleep by night and rise by day, and the seed would sprout and grow" (Mark 4:26–27).

The kingdom of God is already present among us, like a seed that is easily overlooked yet silently takes root. Those to whom the Holy Spirit grants keen vision can see it blossoming. They do not let themselves be robbed of the joy of the kingdom by the weeds that spring up all around.

### *The horizons of the Spirit*

Hope based on the good news which is Jesus himself makes us raise our eyes to contemplate the Lord in the liturgical celebration of the ascension. Even though the Lord may now appear more distant, the horizons of hope expand all the more. In Christ, who brings our human nature to heaven, every man and woman can now freely "enter the sanctuary by the blood of Jesus, by the new and living way he opened for us through the curtain, that is, through his flesh" (Heb 10:19–20). By "the power of the Holy Spirit" we can be witnesses and communicators of a new and redeemed humanity "even to the ends of the earth" (Acts 1:7–8).

Confidence in the seed of God's kingdom and in the mystery of Easter should also shape the way we communicate. This confidence enables us to carry out our work—in all the different ways that communication takes place nowadays—with the conviction that it is possible to recognize and highlight the good news present in every story and in the face of each person.

Those who, in faith, entrust themselves to the guidance of the Holy Spirit realize how God is present and at work in every moment of our lives and history, patiently bringing to pass a history of salvation. Hope is the thread with which this sacred history is woven, and its weaver is none other than the Holy Spirit, the Comforter. Hope is the humblest of virtues, for it remains hidden in the recesses of life; yet it is like the yeast that leavens all the dough. We nurture it by reading ever anew the

Gospel, "reprinted" in so many editions in the lives of the saints who became icons of God's love in this world. Today too, the Spirit continues to sow in us a desire for the kingdom, thanks to all those who, drawing inspiration from the Good News amid the dramatic events of our time, shine like beacons in the darkness of this world, shedding light along the way and opening ever new paths of confidence and hope.

## The Seed of the Word (4:3–39)[2]

Jesus tells a parable to help us grasp the importance of the gift of fortitude. A sower goes out to sow. However, not all of the seed that he sows bears fruit. What falls along the path is eaten by birds; what falls on rocky ground or among brambles springs up but is soon scorched by the sun or choked by thorns. Only what falls on good soil is able to grow and bear fruit (cf. Mark 4:3–9; Matt 13:3–9; Luke 8:4–8). As Jesus explains to his disciples, this sower represents the Father, who abundantly sows the seed of his Word. The seed, however, often meets with the aridity of our heart, which, even when it receives the seed, often is likely to remain barren. However, through the gift of fortitude, the Holy Spirit liberates the soil of our heart. He frees it from sluggishness, from uncertainty, and from all the fears that can hinder it, so that Lord's Word may be put into practice authentically and with joy. The gift of fortitude is a true help; it gives us strength, and it also frees us from so many obstacles.

There are also difficult moments and extreme situations in which the gift of fortitude manifests itself in an extraordinary, exemplary way. This is the case with those who are facing particularly harsh and painful situations that disrupt their lives and those of their loved ones. The Church shines with the testimony of so many brothers and sisters who have not hesitated to give their very lives in order to remain faithful to the Lord and his Gospel. Even today, there is no shortage of Christians who, in many parts of the world, continue to celebrate and bear witness to their faith with deep conviction and serenity and persist even when they know that this may involve them in paying a higher price. We too, all of us, know people who have experienced difficult situations and great suffering. Let us think of those men and women who have a difficult life, who fight to feed their family and to educate their children. They do this because the spirit of fortitude is helping them. How many men and women there are—we do not know their names—who honor our people, who honor our Church, because they are strong: strong in carrying forward their lives, their families, their work, their faith. These brothers and sisters of ours are saints, everyday hidden saints among us. The gift of fortitude enables them to carry on with their duties as individuals, fathers, mothers, brothers, sisters, and citizens. We have many of them! Let us thank the Lord for these Christians who live in hidden holiness. The Holy Spirit is within them, carrying them forward! And it will benefit us to think about these people. If they do all of this, if they can do it, why can't I? It is also good to ask the Lord to give us the gift of fortitude.

We need not think that the gift of fortitude is necessary only on some occasions or in particular situations. This gift must constitute the tenor of our Christian life, *in the ordinary daily routine*. As I said, we need to be strong every day of our lives, to carry forward our life, our family, our faith. The apostle Paul said: "I can do all things in him who strengthens me" (Phil 4:13). When we face daily life—when difficulties arise—let us remember this: "I can do all things in him who strengthens me." The Lord always strengthens us. The Lord does not try us beyond our possibilities. He is always with us. "I can do all things in him who strengthens me."

## Christian Witness (4:21–25)[3]

After speaking of the seed that manages to bear fruit and of those seeds that, after falling on poor soil, cannot bear fruit, Jesus tells us of the lamp, which is not to be placed under a bushel but on a lampstand. This is light, and the Gospel of John tells us that the mystery of God is light and that the light came into the world, but the darkness did not welcome it. It is a light, he added, that should not be hidden but that serves to illuminate.

Here then, is one of the features of a Christian who has received the light in baptism and must give it. A Christian is a witness. Indeed, a Christian can't but show the light he bears within. If a Christian prefers his own darkness to God's light, then something is missing. Darkness enters his heart, because he is afraid of the light. A Christian is a witness, a witness to Jesus Christ, the light of God. And he must place that light in the lampstand of his life.

The gospel passage proposed for the day's liturgy also speaks of *measure*. It reads: "The measure you give will be the measure you get, and still more will be given you" (v. 24). This is the other particular aspect, the other approach typical of a Christian—magnanimity, because a Christian is the child of a magnanimous father with a great spirit.

So too when he says, "Give and you shall be given," the measure that Jesus speaks of is full, good, and overflowing. Similarly, the Christian heart is magnanimous. It is open, always. It is not, therefore, a heart that withdraws into its own selfishness, nor is it a heart that sets limits, that counts: up to here, up to there. When you enter into this light of Jesus, when you enter into Jesus's friendship, when you let the Holy Spirit guide you, your heart becomes open, magnanimous. At that point, a particular dynamic is triggered. A Christian doesn't gain: he loses. But in reality, he loses in order to gain something else, and with this "defeat" of interests, he gains Jesus. A Christian's gain is in becoming a witness to Jesus.

## Jesus Makes the Seed Grow (4:26–28)[4]

It is important to let the Gospel teach us the way of proclamation. At times, even with the best intentions, we can indulge in a certain hunger for power, proselytism, or intolerant fanaticism. Yet the Gospel tells us to reject the idolatry of power and success, undue concern for structures, and a kind of anxiety that has more to do with the spirit of conquest than with the spirit of service. The seed of the kingdom, however tiny, unseen, and at times insignificant, silently continues to grow, thanks to God's tireless activity. "The kingdom of God is as if someone would scatter seed on the ground, and would sleep and rise night and day, and the seed would sprout and grow, he does not know how" (Mark 4:26–27). This is our first reason for confidence: God surpasses all our expectations and constantly surprises us with his generosity. He makes our efforts bear fruit beyond all human calculation.

With this confidence born of the Gospel, we become open to the silent working of the Spirit, which is the basis of mission. There can be no promotion of vocations or Christian mission apart from constant contemplative prayer. The Christian life needs to be nourished by attentive listening to God's word and, above all, by the cultivation of a personal relationship with the Lord in eucharistic adoration, the privileged "place" for our encounter with God.

## The Freedom of the Word (4:26–29)[5]

God's word is unpredictable in its power. The Gospel speaks of a seed which, once sown, grows by itself, even as the farmer sleeps (cf. Mark 4:26–29). The Church has to accept this unruly freedom of the word, which accomplishes what it wills in ways that surpass our calculations and ways of thinking.

## The Kingdom of God (4:26–34)[6]

In today's gospel passage, Jesus speaks to the crowd about the kingdom of God and the dynamics of its growth, and he does so by recounting two brief parables. In the first parable (cf. vv. 26–29), the kingdom of God is compared to the mysterious growth of the seed, which is cast upon the ground and then sprouts, grows, and produces ears of grain, independent of the care of the farmer who, when the seed is fully grown, sees to its harvest. This is the message of the parable: through Jesus's teaching and action, the kingdom of God is proclaimed, bursts into the field of the world and, like the seed, grows and develops by itself, through its own strength and for reasons that are humanly incomprehensible. In its growth and development through history, it does not depend much on humanity, but is above all an expression of the power and goodness of God, of the strength of the Holy Spirit who brings forth Christian life in the people of God.

At times history, with its events and its protagonists, seems to go in the opposite direction of the design of the heavenly Father, who wants justice, fraternity, and peace for all his children. But we are called to live out these periods as seasons of trial, of hope, and of vigilant expectation of the harvest. Indeed, yesterday—like today—the kingdom of God grows in the world in mysterious and surprising ways, revealing the hidden power of the little seed, its victorious vitality. Within the folds of personal and social events, which at times seem to signal the failure of hope, it is important to remain confident in God's subdued but powerful way of acting. For this reason, in moments of darkness and of difficulty we must not lose heart, but remain anchored in faithfulness to God, to his ever-saving presence. Remember this: God always saves. He is the Savior.

In the second parable (cf. vv. 30–32), Jesus compares the kingdom of God to a mustard seed. It is a very small seed, yet it grows to become the greatest of all the plants in the garden. That growth is unforeseeable and surprising. It is not easy for us to enter the logic of the unforeseeable nature of God's action and to accept it in our life. But today the Lord invites us to have an attitude of faith that exceeds all our plans, our calculations, our predictions. God is always the God of surprises. The Lord always surprises us. It is an invitation to open ourselves more generously to God's plans, both on the personal and on the communal level. In our communities, it is important to pay attention to the small and large occasions of goodness that the Lord offers us, allowing ourselves to engage in his dynamics of love, of welcoming, and of mercy toward others.

The authenticity of the Church's mission does not come through success or through the gratification of results, but through going forth with the courage of trust and the humility of abandonment to God—going forth professing Jesus and with the power of the Holy Spirit. It comes through having an awareness of being small and weak instruments that, in God's hands and with his grace, can accomplish great deeds in advancing his kingdom, which is "righteousness and peace and joy in the Holy Spirit" (Rom 14:17).

## God Loves Surprises (4:30–32)[7]

Children, who have no problem understanding God, have much to teach us. They tell us that he accomplishes great things in those who put up no resistance to him, who are simple and sincere, without duplicity. The Gospel shows us how great wonders are accomplished with small things: with a few loaves and two fishes (cf. Matt 14:15–20), with a tiny mustard seed (cf. Mark 4:30–32), with a grain of wheat that dies in the earth (cf. John 12:24), with the gift of just a single glass of water (cf. Matt 10:42), with the two coins of a poor widow (cf. Luke 21:1–4), and with the humility of Mary, the servant of the Lord (cf. Luke 1:46–55).

This is the surprising greatness of God, of a God who is full of surprises and who loves surprises. Let us always keep alive the desire for and trust in God's surprises! These will help us to remember that we are constantly and primarily his children—not masters of our lives, but children of the Father; not autonomous and self-sufficient adults, but children who always need to be lifted up and embraced, who need love and forgiveness.

## God Comes as the Smallest of Seeds (4:31–32)[8]

It is particularly striking how the coming of God into history took place: he was "born of a woman." There was no triumphal entrance or striking epiphany of the Almighty. He did not reveal himself as a brilliantly rising sun but entered the world in the simplest of ways, as a child from his mother, with that "style" that scripture tells us is like rainfall upon the land (cf. Isa 55:10), like the smallest of seeds that sprouts and grows (cf. Mark 4:31–32). Thus, contrary to our expectations, and perhaps even our desires, the kingdom of God, now as then, "is not coming with things that can be observed" (Luke 17:20) but rather in littleness, in humility.

# 5
# The Miracles of Jesus

## Jesus Gazes on Us (5:21–43)[1]

Jesus is always in the midst of the crowd. In this gospel passage, the word "crowd" is repeated at least three times. It isn't an orderly "procession of people," with guards forming a security detail so that the people do not touch Jesus. It is instead a crowd that is pressing around him, enveloping him.... Moreover, every time Jesus went out, there was a greater crowd.

Perhaps a journalist could have written: "The popularity of Rabbi Jesus is falling." But Jesus was seeking something else; he was seeking people. And the people were seeking him. The people had their eyes fixed on him, and he had his eyes fixed on the people.

One could argue that Jesus turned his gaze on the people, on the crowd. But instead, he gazed upon each one. This is the particular thing about Jesus's gaze. Jesus does not depersonalize people: Jesus looks at each one. The proof is found many times in the Gospel narratives. In today's Gospel, for example, we read that Jesus asks: "Who touched me?" when he was in the midst of those people who were pressing around him. It seemed like such a strange question that the disciples said to him, "You see the crowd pressing around you!" They were disconcerted. They must have thought: *Perhaps Jesus didn't sleep well. Perhaps he is mistaken.* But Jesus was certain: "Someone touched me!" In fact, in the midst of that crowd, Jesus realized that the old woman had touched him. And he healed her. There were many people there, but he paid attention to her, a woman; a small old lady.

The gospel narrative continues with the episode of Jairus, who was told his daughter had died. Jesus reassured him: "Do not fear, only believe," and he added, with words he had used with the woman earlier, "Your faith has made you well!" In this situation, too, Jesus was in the midst of the crowd, with many people who were weeping, crying out at the deathbed vigil. In fact, at that time it was common to "hire" women to weep and cry at a vigil. To feel the pain... And to them Jesus said: "Be calm. The girl is sleeping." Perhaps those people, too, may have thought: *This man didn't sleep well*, because they derided him. But Jesus entered and revived the child. The thing to note is that, in all the confusion with the women crying and weeping, Jesus said to the father and mother: "Give her something to eat!" This shows Jesus's attention to the "small things," his gaze at the small things. Didn't he have other matters to concern himself with? No, only this!

In spite of the statisticians who could have said, "The popularity of Rabbi Jesus continues to fall," the Lord preached for hours and the people listened to him; he spoke to each one. And how do we know that he spoke to each one? Because he was aware, he observed that the girl was hungry and he said: "Give her something to eat!"

Also at Nain, there was a crowd following him. And Jesus saw a funeral procession coming out, It was for a young man, a widowed mother's only son. Once again, the Lord is aware of "the small things." Among so many people, he stops the procession, revives the young man, and gives him back to his mother.

Again, in Jericho, when Jesus enters the city, there are people shouting: "The Lord lives! Long live Jesus! Long live the Messiah!" There is a great racket.... A blind man also begins to cry out, and Jesus, despite the great racket, hears the blind man. The Lord is aware of the small details and turns his gaze to the blind man.

All this is to say that Jesus's gaze goes to the great and the small. He looks at all of us, but in particular he looks at each one of us. He looks at our big problems, our great joys; and he also looks at our small things, because he is near. This is how Jesus looks at us.

The author of the Letter to the Hebrews recommends that we run with perseverance... looking to Jesus, with our gaze fixed on him (cf. Heb 12:1–4). But what will happen to us if we do this, if we keep our gaze fixed on Jesus? What will happen to us is what happened to the people after the girl was raised: "They were overcome with amazement." In fact, it so happens that when I go, look at Jesus, walk ahead, fix my gaze on Jesus, what do I find? That he has fixed his gaze on me. This experience is amazing. It is the amazement of the encounter with Jesus. To experience it, however, one need not fear, just as that old lady wasn't afraid to go and touch the hem of his cloak. And so, let us not be afraid! Let us run along this path, with our gaze always fixed on Jesus. And we will have this beautiful surprise: it will fill us with amazement. Jesus himself has fixed his gaze on me.

## The Gospel in Hand (5:21–43)[2]

The author of the Letter to the Hebrews refers to the memory of those first days after his conversion, after his encounter with

Jesus, and he recalls the witness of our fathers, how much they suffered when they were on the journey. The author notes that we, too, are surrounded by a great cloud of witnesses. He also recalls our experience, when we were so happy in our first encounter with Jesus. This is the memory that serves as a point of reference for Christian life.

But today, the author of the letter speaks about hope. He tells us that we must have the courage to go forward, we must persevere in running the race that lies before us. Then he notes that the very core of hope is keeping our eyes fixed on Jesus. In fact, if we don't keep our eyes fixed on Jesus, it is difficult for us to have hope. We can perhaps be optimistic, be positive, but do we have hope?

After all, hope is learned only by looking to Jesus, contemplating him through contemplative prayer. I can ask you: How do you pray? Someone might respond: "Father, I say the prayers I learned as a child." Okay, this is good. Someone else might add: "I pray the rosary, too, every day!" It's good to pray the rosary every day. And finally, one might say: "I also talk with the Lord, when I have a problem, or with Our Lady or with the saints." And this is good, too.

Faced with all this, I ask another question: "Do you pray in contemplation?" The question might be unsettling, and someone might ask: "What is this, Father? What is this prayer? Where can we buy it? How do we do it?" It can be done only with the Gospel in hand. Basically, you pick up the Gospel, select a passage, read it once, read it twice. Imagine, as if you see what is happening, and contemplate Jesus.

Take, for example, a passage from the Gospel according to Mark (5:21–43). Beginning with this page, I ask: "How do I contemplate with today's Gospel?" I see that Jesus was in the midst of the crowd; there was a great crowd around him. The word "crowd" is used five times in this passage. But doesn't Jesus rest? I imagine so, but always with the crowd! Most of Jesus's life is spent on the street, with the crowd. Doesn't he rest? Yes, once: the Gospel says that he slept on the boat, but the storm came and the disciples woke him. Jesus was constantly among the people.

For this reason, we look to Jesus this way. I contemplate Jesus this way, I imagine Jesus this way. And I say to Jesus whatever comes to my mind to say to him.

Then, in the midst of the crowd, there was that sick woman, and Jesus was aware. But how did Jesus, in the middle of so many people, realize that a woman had touched him? And, indeed, he asked directly: "Who touched me?" This question tells us that Jesus not only understands the crowd, feels the crowd, but he hears the beating of each one of our hearts, of each one of us: he cares for all and for each one, always!

### *The cure of Jairus's daughter*

The same situation happens again when the ruler of the synagogue approaches Jesus to tell him about his gravely ill little daughter. And Jesus leaves everything to tend to her: Jesus in the great and in the small, always! Then, we can go on and see that he arrives at the house, he sees that tumult, the women who were called to mourn over the dead body, wailing, weeping. Jesus says: "Don't worry: she's sleeping!" But in response to these words, some even begin to scoff at him. However, "he stays quiet," and with his patience he manages to bear this situation, to avoid responding to those who mock him.

The gospel account culminates with the girl's resurrection. And Jesus, rather than saying: "Praised be God!" says to them: "Please, give her something to eat," for Jesus always has the fine details in front of him.

### *Contemplative prayer*

What I did with this Gospel is contemplative prayer: to pick up the Gospel, read, and imagine myself in the scene, imagine what's happening and speak with Jesus about what comes from my heart. This form of prayer allows hope to grow because we have our eyes fixed on Jesus. Pray in contemplation. Even if we have many commitments, we can always find the time, even fifteen minutes at home, to pick up the Gospel, a short passage, imagine what is happening, and talk to Jesus about it. Then our eyes will be fixed on Jesus, and not so much on soap operas, for example. Our ears will be fixed on the words of Jesus and not so much on the neighbors' gossip.

Contemplative prayer helps us to hope and teaches us to live from the substance of the Gospel. And this is why we must always pray: say prayers, pray the rosary, speak with the Lord, but also carry out this contemplative prayer in order to keep our eyes fixed on Jesus. From here comes hope. And also, our Christian life moves within this framework, between memory and hope: the memory of the entire past journey, the memory of so many graces received from the Lord; and hope, looking to the Lord, who is the only One who can give me hope. And to look to the Lord—to know the Lord—we pick up the Gospel and pray in contemplation.

## The Two Men Who Are Fathers (5:21–43)[3]

Jairus, one of the synagogue's leaders during the time of Jesus, who goes to ask for his daughter to be restored to health, and David, who suffers over the war led by his son, show how every father receives a kind of unction from his child: he cannot understand himself without his son.

Even though David's son Absalom had become his enemy, David waited for news of the war. He sat between the two gates of the palace and watched. Everyone thought that he was waiting for news of a great victory, but instead he was waiting for something else: he was waiting for his child. He was concerned for his child. He was the king, he was the leader of the country, but first and foremost he was a father. And so when the news came of his son's death, David was deeply shaken. He went up to the floor above the door and cried: "My son Absalom! My son, my son Absalom! If only I had died instead of you, Absalom, my son, my son!"

This is the heart of a father who never disowns his son; even if he is a thief—even if he is an enemy—the father cries for him. In the Bible, David weeps for his children on two occasions: on this occasion and when death was coming to the son who had been conceived in adultery. In that instance, he fasted and did penance in order to save his son's life because he was his father.

There is another element of this scene: silence. The soldiers have returned from battle to the city in silence. In contrast, when David was young and returned to the city after killing the Philistine, women came out from their homes to praise him, rejoicing; this is how soldiers returned after a victory. Instead, on the occasion of Absalom's death, victory was not visible because the king was crying. More than being a king and a victor, David was a grieving father.

As for the figure in the gospel passage, the leader of the synagogue was an important person, but when faced with his daughter's illness, he was not ashamed to throw himself at Jesus's feet and beg him: "My daughter is dying. Come and lay your hands upon her that she might be saved and live!" The man does not reflect on the consequences of what he is doing. He does not stop to wonder whether Christ is a sorcerer rather than a prophet, and he risks looking like a fool. Being a father, he does not reflect. He risks throwing himself before Jesus and he pleads. In this scene, the figures enter the house to find crying and screaming. There were people shouting loudly because that was their job: their job was to go and cry in the homes of the dead. But theirs were not the cries of a father.

The priority of the two fathers was their children. This brings to mind the first thing we say about God in the Creed: "I believe in God the Father." We recall God's paternity and that this is how God is with us. Some might say: "But Father, God does not cry!" But of course he does! We remember how Jesus cried as he looked at Jerusalem: "Jerusalem, Jerusalem, how many times I wished to gather your children like a hen that gathers her chicks under her wings." Therefore, God does cry. Jesus wept for us. And in his weeping, we see the cries of a father who wants everyone to be with him in times of difficulty.

In the Bible, there are at least two unpleasant instances in which the father responds to the cries of his child. The first is the story of Isaac, who is led by Abraham to his death as a burnt offering. Isaac realizes that he is bringing the wood and the fire, but not the sheep for the sacrifice. And so with anguish in his heart he says, "Father"—to which immediately comes the reply: "I am here, son." The second instance is that of Jesus in the Garden of Olives. With anguish in his heart, he says: "Father, if it is possible let this cup pass from me." And the angels come to give him strength. This is how our God is: he is a father.

### *The father waits*

The image of David sitting between the two gates of the palace, awaiting the news, brings to mind a parable in chapter 15 of Luke's Gospel, the parable of the father awaiting the prodigal son who had fled with all of his money, all of his inheritance. And yet, still the father waited for him. Scripture tells us that the father saw him from afar because he had been waiting every day for his son to return. In that merciful father, we see our God, who is our father. From this springs the hope that the fathers of families and spiritual fathers—religious, priests, and bishops—can increasingly be like the two characters in the readings: the two men who are fathers.

Meditate on these two images: David who wept and the leader of the synagogue who, without shame or fear of ridicule, threw himself before Jesus because his child's life was at stake. We each need to ask the Holy Spirit to teach us how to say "Abba, Father," because it is a grace to call God "Father" from the heart.

## Faith Gives Life (5:21–43)[4]

The Gospel presents the account of the resurrection of a young twelve-year-old girl, the daughter of one of the leaders of the synagogue, who falls at Jesus's feet and beseeches him: "My little daughter is at the point of death. Come and lay your hands on her, so that she may be made well, and live" (Mark 5:23). In this prayer, we hear the concern of every father for the life and well-being of his child. We also hear the great faith that this man has in Jesus. And when news arrives that the little girl is dead, Jesus tells him: "Do not fear, only believe" (v. 36). These words from Jesus give us courage! And he frequently also says them to us: "Do not fear, only believe." Entering the house, the Lord sends away all those who are weeping and wailing and turns to the dead girl, saying: "Little girl, I say to you, arise" (v. 41). And immediately, the little girl gets up and begins to walk. Here we see Jesus's absolute power over death, which for him is like a dream from which one can awaken.

The evangelist inserts another episode in this account: the healing of a woman who had been bleeding for twelve years. Because of this ailment, which, according to the culture of the time, rendered her "impure," she was forced to avoid all human contact. The poor woman was condemned to a living death. In the midst of the crowd following Jesus, this unknown woman says to herself: "If I touch even his garments, I shall be made well" (v. 28). And thus it happened. The need to be freed urges her to dare, and her faith "snatches" healing from the Lord. She who believes "touches" Jesus and draws saving grace from him. This is faith: to touch Jesus is to draw from him the grace that saves. It saves us, it saves our spiritual life, and it saves us from so many problems. Jesus notices and, in the midst of the people, looks for the woman's face. She steps forward trembling and he says to her: "Daughter, your faith has made you well" (v. 34). It is the voice of the heavenly Father who speaks in Jesus: "Daughter, you are not cursed, you are not excluded, you are my child!" And every time Jesus approaches us, when we go forth from him with faith, we sense this from the Father: "Child, you are my son, you are my daughter! You are healed. I forgive everyone for everything. I heal all people and all things."

These two episodes—a healing and a resurrection—share one core idea: *faith*. The message is clear, and it can be summed up in one question: *Do we believe that Jesus can heal us and can raise us from the dead?* The entire Gospel is written in the light of this faith: Jesus is risen, he has conquered death, and by his victory we too will rise again. This faith, which for the first Christians was certain, can become tarnished and uncertain, to the point that some may confuse resurrection with reincarnation. The word of God today invites us to live in the certainty of the resurrection: Jesus is the Lord, Jesus has power over evil and over death, and he wants to lead us to the house of the Father where life reigns. And there we will all meet again, all of us here in this square today, we will meet again in the house of the Father, in the life that Jesus will give us.

The resurrection of Christ acts in history as the source of renewal and hope. Anyone who is desperate and exhausted, if he entrusts himself to Jesus and to his love, can begin to live again. And to begin a new life, to change life, is a way of rising again, of resurrecting. Faith is a force of life; it gives fullness to our humanity, and those who believe in Christ must acknowledge this in order to promote life in every situation, in order to let everyone, especially the weakest, experience the love of God who frees and saves.

Let us ask the Lord, through the intercession of the Virgin Mary, for the gift of a strong and courageous faith that will urge us to spread hope and life among our brothers and sisters.

## The Balm of Mercy (5:25–35)[5]

The works of mercy are closely linked to the "spiritual senses." In our prayer, we ask for the grace to "feel and savor" the Gospel so that it can make us more sensitive in our lives. Moved by the Spirit and led by Jesus, we can see from afar, with the eyes of mercy, those who have fallen along the wayside. We can hear the cries of Bartimaeus and feel with Jesus the timid yet determined gesture of the woman suffering from a hemorrhage as she touches his robe. We can ask for the grace to taste with the crucified Jesus the bitter gall of all those who share in his cross, and smell the stench of misery—in field hospitals, in trains, and in boats crammed with people. The balm of mercy does not disguise this stench. Rather, by anointing it, it awakens new hope.

## Loving Kindness (5:41)[6]

To be open to a genuine encounter with others, "a kind look" is essential. This is incompatible with a negative attitude that readily points out other people's shortcomings while overlooking one's own. A kind look helps us to see beyond our own limitations, to be patient and to cooperate with others despite our differences. Loving kindness builds bonds, cultivates relationships, creates new networks of integration, and knits a firm social fabric. Without a sense of belonging we cannot sustain a commitment to others; we end up seeking our convenience alone, and life in common becomes impossible. Antisocial persons think that others exist only for the satisfaction of their own needs. Consequently, there is no room for the gentleness of love and its expression. Those who love are capable of speaking words of comfort, strength, consolation, and encouragement. These were the words that Jesus himself spoke: "Take heart, my son!" (Matt 9:2); "Great is your faith!" (Matt 15:28); "Arise!" (Mark 5:41); "Go in peace" (Luke 7:50); "Be not afraid" (Matt 14:27). These are not words that demean, sadden, anger, or show scorn. In our families, we must learn to imitate Jesus's own gentleness in our way of speaking to one another.

## The Sensitivity of Mercy (5:41–43)[7]

I have always been struck by the passage of the Lord's encounter with the woman caught in adultery, and how, by refusing to condemn her, he "fell short of" the law. In response to the question they asked to test him—"Should she be stoned or not?"—Jesus did not make a judgment; he did not apply the law. He played dumb—here, too, the Lord has something to teach us!—and focused on something else. He thus initiated a process in the heart of the woman who needed to hear those words: "Neither do I condemn you." He stretched out his hand and helped her to her feet, letting her see a gentle gaze that changed her heart. The Lord took the daughter of Jairus by the hand and said: "Give her something to eat." He raised the son of the widow of Nain and gave him back to his mother. And here he tells the sinful woman to rise. He puts us exactly where God wants us to be: standing, on our feet, never down on the ground.

Sometimes I feel saddened and annoyed when people go straight to the last words Jesus speaks to her: "Go and sin no more." They use these words to "defend" Jesus from bypassing the law. I believe that his words are of a piece with his actions. He bends down to write on the ground as a prelude to what he is about to say to those who want to stone the woman, and he does so again before talking to her. This tells us something about the time that the Lord takes in judging and forgiving, the time he gives each person to look into his or her own heart and then to walk away.

In talking to the woman, the Lord opens other spaces: *one is that of non-condemnation*. The Gospel clearly mentions this open space. It makes us see things through the eyes of Jesus, who tells us: "I see no one else but this woman."

Then Jesus has the woman herself look around. He asks her: "Where are those who condemned you?" (The word "condemn" is important, since it is about what we find unacceptable about those who judge or caricature us.) Once he has opened before her eyes this space freed of other people's judgments, he tells her that neither will he throw a stone: "Nor do I condemn you." Then he opens up another free space before her: "Go and sin no more." His command has to do with the future, to help her to make a new start and to "walk in love." Such is the sensitivity of mercy; it looks with compassion on the past and offers encouragement for the future.

Those words, "Go and sin no more," are not easy. The Lord says them "with her." He helps her put into words what she herself feels, a free "no" to sin that is like Mary's "yes" to grace. That "no" has to be said to the deeply rooted sin present in everyone. In that woman, it was a social sin; people approached her either to sleep with her or to throw stones at her. There was no other way to approach her. That is why the Lord does not only clear the path before her but sets her on her way, so that she can stop being the "object" of other people's gaze and instead take control of her life.

Those words, "sin no more," refer not only to morality but also to a kind of sin that keeps her from living her life. Jesus also told the paralytic at Bethesda to sin no more (cf. John 5:14). But that man had justified himself with all the sad things that had "happened to him"; unlike the woman, he suffered from a victim complex. So Jesus challenged him ever so slightly by saying: "... lest something worse happen to you." The Lord took advantage of his way of thinking, his fears, to draw him out of his paralysis. He gave him a little scare, we might say. The point is that each of us has to hear the words "sin no more" in his or her own deeply personal way.

This image of the Lord who sets people on their way is very typical. He is the God who walks at his people's side, who leads them forward, who accompanies our history. Hence, the object of his mercy is quite clear: it is everything that keeps a man or a woman from walking on the right path, that keeps them from walking with their own people, at their own pace, to where God is asking them to go. What troubles him is that people get lost, or fall behind, or try to go it on their own. That they end up nowhere. That they are not there for the Lord, ready to go wherever he wants to send them. That they do not walk humbly before him (cf. Mic 6:8). That they do not walk in love (cf. Eph 5:2).

6

# The Ministry of Jesus

## The Rejection (6:2–3)[1]

No family can be fruitful if it sees itself as overly different or "set apart." To avoid this risk, we should remember that Jesus's own family, so full of grace and wisdom, did not appear unusual or different from others. That is why people found it hard to acknowledge Jesus's wisdom: "Where did this man get all this? Is not this the carpenter, the son of Mary?" (Mark 6:2–3). "Is this not the carpenter's son?" (Matt 13:55). These questions make clear that theirs was an ordinary family, close to others, a normal part of the community. Jesus did not grow up in a narrow and stifling relationship with Mary and Joseph, but readily interacted with the wider family, the relatives of his parents and their friends. This explains how, on returning from Jerusalem, Mary and Joseph could imagine for a whole day that the twelve-year-old Jesus was somewhere in the caravan, listening to people's stories and sharing their concerns: "Supposing him to be in the group of travelers, they went a day's journey" (Luke 2:44). Still, some Christian families, whether because of the language they use, the way they act or treat others, or their constant harping on the same two or three issues end up being seen as remote and not really part of the community; even their relatives feel looked down upon or judged by them.

## Jesus, the Carpenter (6:3)[2]

Jesus lived in full harmony with creation, and others were amazed: "What sort of man is this, that even the winds and the sea obey him?" (Matt 8:27). His appearance was not that of an ascetic set apart from the world, nor of an enemy to the pleasant things of life. Of himself he said: "The Son of Man came eating and drinking and they say, 'Look, a glutton and a drunkard!'" (Matt 11:19). He was far removed from philosophies that despised the body, matter, and the things of the world. Such unhealthy dualisms, nonetheless, left a mark on certain Christian thinkers in the course of history and disfigured the Gospel. Jesus worked with his hands, in daily contact with the matter created by God, to which he gave form by his craftsmanship. It is striking that most of his life was dedicated to this task in a simple life that awakened no admiration at all: "Is not this the carpenter, the son of Mary?" (Mark 6:3). In this way, he sanctified human labor and endowed it with a special significance for our development. As Saint John Paul II taught, "By enduring the toil of work in union with Christ crucified for us, man in a way collaborates with the Son of God for the redemption of humanity."

## The Profile of an Apostle (6:7–13)[3]

We have heard how Jesus called his disciples and sent them to proclaim the Gospel: it is he who calls. The Gospel recounts that he called them to him, sent them, and gave them power. In the vocation of the disciples, the Lord gives power—the power to cast out impure spirits, to liberate, to heal. This is the power that Jesus gives. Indeed, he does not give the power to maneuver or to build large companies. Instead he gives the same power that he had; the power that he received from the Father, he conveys to them. And he does so with plain advice: go into the community, but do not take anything for the journey except a staff: no bread, no bag, no money... in poverty!

The Gospel is so very rich and powerful that it does not need to create large firms or big companies in order to be proclaimed. The Gospel should be proclaimed in poverty, and a real pastor is one who goes like Jesus—poor, to proclaim the Gospel with that power. And when the Gospel is safeguarded with this simplicity, with this poverty, one clearly sees that salvation is not a theology of prosperity but rather a gift, the same gift that Jesus received in order to give.

Let's recall that beautiful scene in the synagogue, when Jesus introduces himself: "I was sent to bring salvation, to bring glad tidings to the poor, liberation to the incarcerated, to the blind the gift of sight. Liberation to all those who are oppressed and to proclaim the year of grace, the year of joy." This is precisely the aim of the gospel message, without many curious, worldly things. This is how Jesus conveys it.

### *The pastoral mission of Jesus*

And what does Jesus command the disciples to do? What is his pastoral plan? It is simply to cure, heal, raise, liberate, and cast out demons: this is the simple plan. It coincides with the mission of the Church, the Church that heals and cures. I have spoken a few times of the Church as a field hospital. It's true! How many wounded there are, how many wounded! How many people who need their wounds to be healed!

This is the Church's mission: healing the wounds of the heart, opening doors, liberating, and saying that God is good, that God forgives all, that God is Father, that God is gentle, that God always waits for us.

According to the Gospel of Luke (10:17–20), the disciples returned with joy from their mission because they hadn't believed they would succeed. And they said to the Lord: "Lord, even the demons left!" They were joyful because this power of Jesus, employed with simplicity, with poverty, and with love, had produced a good result.

The very phrase that Jesus addressed to the joyful disciples, according to the Gospel, explains everything. They recounted: "We did this, and this, and this, and this. . . ." After listening to them, Jesus closed his eyes and said: "I saw Satan fall like lightning from heaven." The words reveal the struggle of the Church. It's true, we should offer help and create aid organizations, for the Lord gives us gifts for this. But when we forget this mission, forget about poverty, forget apostolic zeal and put our hope in these means, the Church slowly changes into an NGO and becomes a fine organization: powerful but not evangelical, because that spirit, that poverty, that healing power is lacking.

There is more. On their return, Jesus brings the disciples with him to rest, to have a day in the country, to have sandwiches and soft drinks. The Lord wants them to spend some time together to celebrate. And together they reflect on the mission they have just completed. But Jesus doesn't tell them: "You're great! Now let's plan things better for the next mission!" He limits himself to recommending: "When you have done all that is commanded you, say, 'We are unworthy servants'" (Luke 17:10).

With these words, the Lord described the profile of an apostle. Indeed, what would have been the greatest praise for an apostle? The answer: He was a laborer for the kingdom, he was a worker for the kingdom. Indeed, this is the highest praise, because the apostle goes on Jesus's path of proclamation; he goes to heal, to safeguard, to proclaim glad tidings, and in this year of grace, he goes to enable the people to find the Father once again, to make peace in the hearts of people.

## Hospitality (6:7–13)[4]

Jesus calls his disciples and sends them out, giving them clear and precise instructions. He challenges them to take on a range of attitudes and ways of acting. Sometimes these can strike us as exaggerated or even absurd. It would be easier to interpret these attitudes symbolically or "spiritually." But Jesus is quite precise, very clear. He doesn't tell them simply to do whatever they think they can.

Let us consider some of these attitudes: "Take nothing for the journey except a staff; no bread, no bag, no money. . . . When you enter a house, stay there until you leave the place" (cf. Mark 6:8–11). All this might seem quite unrealistic.

We could concentrate on the words, "bread," "money," "bag," "staff," "sandals," and "tunic." And this would be fine, but it strikes me that there is one key word can easily pass unnoticed among these challenging words. It is a word at the heart of Christian spirituality, of our experience of discipleship: "welcome." Jesus as the good master, the good teacher, sends them out to be welcomed, to experience hospitality. He says to them: "Where you enter a house, stay there." He sends them out to learn one of the hallmarks of the community of believers. We might say that a Christian is someone who has learned to welcome others, who has learned to show hospitality.

Jesus does not send them out as men of influence, landlords, or officials armed with rules and regulations. Instead, he makes them see that the Christian journey is simply about changing hearts: one's own heart, first, and then helping to transform the hearts of others. It is about learning to live differently, under a different law, with different rules. It is about turning from the path of selfishness, conflict, division, and superiority, and taking instead the path of life, generosity, and love. It is about passing from a mentality that dominates, stifles, and manipulates to a mentality that welcomes, accepts, and cares.

These are two contrasting mentalities, two ways of approaching our life and our mission. How many times do we see mission in terms of plans and programs? How many times do we see evangelization as involving any number of strategies, tactics, maneuvers, and techniques, as if we could convert people on the basis of our own arguments? Today, the Lord says to us quite clearly: in the mentality of the Gospel, you do not convince people with arguments, strategies, or tactics. You convince them by simply learning how to welcome them.

### *The home of hospitality*

The Church is a mother with an open heart. She knows how to welcome and accept, especially those in need of greater care, those in greater difficulty. The Church, as desired by Jesus, is the home of hospitality. And how much good we can do if only we try to speak this language of hospitality, this language of receiving and welcoming. How much pain can be soothed, how much despair can be allayed in a place where we feel at home! This requires open doors, especially the doors of our heart; welcoming the hungry, the thirsty, the stranger, the naked, the sick, the prisoner (cf. Matt 25:34–37), the leper, and the paralytic; welcoming those who do not think as we do, who do not have faith or who have lost it—and sometimes, we have been to blame; welcoming the persecuted, the unemployed; welcoming those from different cultures, of which our earth is so richly blessed; and welcoming sinners, because each one of us is also a sinner.

So often we forget that there is an evil that underlies our sins, that precedes our sins. There is a bitter root that causes damage, great damage, and silently destroys so many lives. There is an evil that gradually finds a place in our hearts and eats away at our life. That evil is isolation. Isolation has many, many causes. It can destroy our life and result in much harm. It makes us turn our backs on others, God, and the community. It closes us in on ourselves. From here we see that the real work of the Church, our mother, should not be mainly about managing works and projects but rather about learning to experience community with others. A welcome-filled community is the best witness that God is our Father, for "by this all will know that you are my disciples, if you have love for one another" (John 13:35).

In this way, Jesus teaches us a new way of thinking. He opens before us a horizon brimming with life, beauty, truth, and fulfillment.

### *Opening horizons*

God never closes off horizons; he is never unconcerned about the lives and sufferings of his children. God never allows himself to be outdone in generosity. So he sends us his Son, he gives him to us, he hands him over, he shares him... so that we can learn the way of fraternity, of self-giving. In a definitive way, he opens up a new horizon. He is a new word that sheds light on so many situations of exclusion, disintegration, loneliness, and isolation. He is a word that breaks the silence of loneliness.

And when we are weary or worn down by our efforts to evangelize, it is good to remember that the life which Jesus holds out to us responds to the deepest needs of people. "We were created for what the Gospel offers us: friendship with Jesus and love of our brothers and sisters" (*Evangelii Gaudium,* 265).

One thing is certain: we cannot force anyone to receive us, to welcome us; this is itself part of our poverty and freedom.

But neither can anyone force us not to be welcoming, hospitable in the lives of our people. No one can tell us not to accept and embrace the lives of our brothers and sisters, especially those who have lost hope and zest for life. How good it would be to think of our parishes, communities, chapels, wherever there are Christians, with open doors, true centers of encounter between ourselves and God.

The Church is a mother, like Mary. In her, we have a model. We too must provide a home, like Mary, who did not lord it over the word of God, but rather welcomed that word, bore it in her womb, and gave it to others.

We too must provide a home, like the earth, which does not choke the seed, but receives it, nourishes it, and makes it grow.

This is how we want to be Christians, how we want to live the faith on this Paraguayan soil, like Mary, accepting and welcoming God's life in our brothers and sisters, in confidence and with the certainty that the Lord will shower blessings and our land will yield its increase. May it be so!

## John the Baptist's Darkest Hour (6:14–29)[5]

The Gospel of Mark (6:14–29) speaks about the imprisonment and martyrdom of John, who was a man faithful to his mission, a man who suffered many temptations and never, ever betrayed his vocation. He was a faithful man of great authority, respected by everyone—the great one of that time.

What came out of his mouth was just. His heart was just. He was so great that Jesus would say that "Elijah returned to clean house, to prepare the way." And John was aware that his duty was simply to proclaim the coming of the Messiah. He was aware, reflecting on what Saint Augustine said, that he was only the voice; the Word was another. And when he was tempted to "steal" this truth, he remained just: "It is not me. He is coming after me. I am the servant; I am the manservant; I am the one who opens the doors, in order that he may come."

### *The precursor*

John is the forerunner. He is the forerunner not only of the Lord's entry into public life but of the entire life of the Lord. The Baptist goes forth on the Lord's path; he bears witness to the Lord not only by indicating—"He is the one!"—but also by leading his life to the end as the Lord did. Through his martyrdom, he became the forerunner of the life and death of Jesus Christ.

The great one suffers so many trials and becomes small, so very small, until scorned. John, like Jesus, abases himself. He knows the way of abasement. John, with all that authority, thinking of his life, comparing it with that of Jesus, tells the people who he is, how his life will be: "It is fitting that he grow; however, I must become small." And this is John's life: to become small before Christ, so that Christ may grow. It is the life of the servant who makes room, makes way for the Lord to come.

John's life was not easy. Indeed, when Jesus began his public life, John was close to the Essenes, that is, to the observers of the law, but also of prayers, of penance. At a certain point, while incarcerated, he suffered the trial of darkness, of his soul's darkest hour. And that scene is moving: John sent two of his disciples to Jesus to ask him: "Are you the one who is to come or shall we look for another?" (Luke 7:19). Thus, along John's path appeared the darkness of mistake, the darkness of life burnt out in error. And for him, this was a cross.

To John's question Jesus responds with the words of Isaiah. The Baptist understands, but his heart remains in darkness. Nevertheless, John agrees to the requests of the king who enjoys listening to him, and who enjoys an adulterous life. John almost becomes a preacher of the court, of this confused king. He humiliates himself because he hopes to convert this man.

Finally, after this purification, after this continuous descent into annihilation, his life ends. That confused king is able to make a decision—not because his heart is converted but rather because wine gives him courage.

And so John's life is ended under the authority of a mediocre, drunken, and corrupt king, because of a daughter's dance and because of the vindictive hatred of an adulterous woman. Thus, the great one—"the greatest man born of woman"—meets his end.

***A story that continues in our martyrs***

When I read this passage, I am moved. I think about two things. First, I think about our martyrs, today's martyrs, those men, women, and children who are persecuted, hated, driven from their homes, tortured, and massacred. And this is not a thing of the past. It is happening today. Our martyrs meet their end under the authority of corrupt people who hate Jesus Christ. For this reason, it will do us good to think about our martyrs. Today, we remember Paul Miki, who died in 1597. Let us think of those of today. . . .

This passage also urges us to reflect on our own life: *I too will meet my end. We all will. No one can "buy" life.* We too, willingly or unwillingly, are traveling the road of life's existential annihilation. And this impels us to pray that this annihilation may resemble as much as possible that of Jesus Christ, his annihilation.

Thus, we have come full circle. John, the great one, who diminishes endlessly into nothingness; the martyrs, who are diminishing today, in our Church today, into nothingness; and we, who are on this road and heading toward the ground, where we will all end up. May the Lord illuminate us, enable us to understand the way of John, the forerunner of Jesus, the way of Jesus who teaches us how ours has to be.

## Return to the First Galilee (6:14–29)[6]

John was a man who had a short life and a short time to announce the Word of God. He was the man God had sent to prepare the way for his Son. But John's death was brutal; he was beheaded at the order of Herod. He became the price of a show for the royal court gathered at a banquet. At the court, many things were acceptable: corruption, vices, and crimes. The court favored these things.

There are three fundamental characteristics that describe Saint John the Baptist. What did John do? First, *he announced the Lord*. He announced that the Savior, the Lord, was coming, that the kingdom of God was near. He proclaimed this forcefully, baptizing and leading people to repentance. John was a strong man who announced Jesus Christ. He was the prophet who was closest to Jesus Christ. He was so close that he himself pointed others to him. In fact, when he saw Jesus he exclaimed: "It is he!"

Second, he did not allow himself to become possessed by his own moral authority, even when the opportunity to say "I am the Messiah" was offered to him. John had *great moral authority*! All the people came to him. The Gospel says that the scribes would approach him to ask, "What should we do?" as did the people and even soldiers. "Repent!" was John's reply, and "Do not steal!"

The Pharisees and doctors of the law also noticed the "strength" of John and could see that he was a righteous man. Because of this, they went to him and asked: "Are you the Messiah?" For John, this was a moment of temptation and vanity. He could have responded: "I cannot speak about this," and in this way he would have been leaving the question open. Or he could have responded: "I do not know…" with false humility.

Instead, John was clear and said: "No, I am not! After me comes one who is mightier than I, the thong of whose sandals I am not worthy to stoop down and untie."

John did not fall into the temptation of stealing the title. He clearly proclaimed, "I am a voice, and nothing more. The Word will come next. I am only a voice!" John did not steal dignity, for he was a man of truth.

Third, John *imitated Christ*; he imitated Jesus. He did this to the point that, in those times, the Pharisees and the doctors of the law believed that he might be the Messiah. Even Herod, who had him killed, believed that John might be the Messiah. This very fact shows the extent to which John followed the way of Jesus, especially in humility. John was humiliated, and humbled himself even to the end, to his death. He went to meet the same shameful death as the Lord Jesus, punished as a robber, a thief, a criminal on a cross. John was the victim of a weak and lustful man, who was pushed by the hatred of an adulteress, on a whim in response to a dancer. John and Jesus suffered humiliating deaths.

Like Jesus, John, too, had his Garden of Gethsemane, his anguish in prison, when he questioned whether or not he was wrong. He sent his disciples to ask Jesus: "Tell me, are you the Messiah or is it someone else and I am wrong?" What he experienced was the "darkness of the soul," the "darkness that purifies." Jesus responded to John in the same way that the Father responded to Jesus: he comforted him. Reflecting on this darkness, we recall the witness of Blessed Teresa of Calcutta. She was a woman who was praised all around the world, and even received the Nobel Prize! But she knew that for a long period of her life, there was only darkness within her. John also experienced this darkness, and through proclaiming Jesus Christ and not taking advantage of the prophecy, he imitated Jesus Christ.

***John: the image and call of a disciple***

In John, therefore, we see the image and the vocation of a disciple. The source of the disciple's behavior can be seen in the Gospel when Mary visits Elizabeth and John dances for joy in his mother's womb. Jesus and John were indeed cousins and perhaps they later found each other, but that first encounter filled John's heart with much joy. This turned him into a disciple, a man who proclaimed Jesus Christ, who did not put himself in Christ's place, but instead followed Christ's path.

Let's do an examination of conscience on our discipleship: Do we announce Jesus Christ? Do we proclaim Jesus Christ? Do we profit from our condition as Christians, as if it were a privilege? It is important, in this regard, to look at the example of John who did not take advantage of the prophecy.

Do we choose the path of Jesus Christ, the way of humiliation, of humility, of abasing ourselves at his service?

If this is not the case, then it is good to ask ourselves: When was my encounter with Jesus Christ, that encounter that filled me with joy? It is a way to return spiritually to that first encounter with the Lord, to return to the first Galilee encounter: we all have one! The secret is to go there, to encounter the Lord again and to continue down this beautiful path on which he must increase and we must decrease.

## Care for Your Priests (6:30)[7]

The first face I ask you as bishops to guard in your hearts is that of your priests. Do not leave them exposed to loneliness and abandonment, easy prey to a worldliness that devours the heart. Be attentive and learn how to read their expressions so as to rejoice with them when they feel the joy of recounting all that they have "done and taught" (Mark 6:30). Also, do not step back when they feel humiliated and can only cry because they "have denied the Lord" (cf. Luke 22:61–62). Why not also offer your support, in communion with Christ, when one of them, already disheartened, goes out with Judas into "the night" (cf. John 13:30). As bishops in these situations, your paternal care for your priests must never be found wanting. Encourage communion among them; seek the perfection of their gifts; involve them in great ventures, for the heart of an apostle was not made for small things.

## The Three Words of the Shepherd (6:30–34)[8]

After the experience of mission, the apostles returned content but also tired. Jesus, filled with understanding, wants to give them some relief, and so he takes them away, to a lonely place, so they can rest a while (cf. Mark 6:31). "Many saw them going, and knew...and got there ahead of them" (v. 33). Here, the evangelist presents the image of Jesus with singular intensity, "photographing," so to speak, his eyes and gathering the sentiments of his heart. The evangelist states: "As he landed he saw a great throng, and he had compassion on them, because they were like sheep without a shepherd; and he began to teach them many things" (v. 34).

Let us recall the three verbs in this evocative scene: *to see, to have compassion,* and *to teach*. We can call them the verbs of the shepherd. The first and second—to see and to have compassion—are always found together in the person of Jesus. In fact, his gaze is not the gaze of a sociologist or a photojournalist, for he always gazes with "the eyes of the heart." These two verbs, to see and to have compassion, are what make Jesus the Good Shepherd. His compassion too is not merely a human feeling, but is the deep emotion of the Messiah in whom God's tenderness is made flesh. From this tenderness is born Jesus's wish to nourish the crowd with the bread of his word, that is, to teach the word of God to the people. Jesus sees, Jesus has compassion, and Jesus teaches us. This is beautiful!

## FEED THE HUNGRY (6:30–44)[9]

The experience of hunger is hard. Those who have endured war or famine know it well. However, this experience is repeated every day, and it coexists alongside abundance and waste. The words of the apostle James are ever timely: "What good is it, my brothers and sisters, if you say you have faith but do not have works? Can faith save you? If a brother or sister is naked and lacks daily food, and one of you says to them, 'Go in peace; keep warm and eat your fill,' and yet you do not supply their bodily needs, what is the good of that? So faith by itself, if it has no works, is dead" (2:14–17) because it is incapable of doing works, of doing charity, of love. There is always someone who is hungry or thirsty and who needs me. I cannot delegate this to another. This poor person needs me, my help, my word, my commitment. We are all involved in this.

### *The lessons of Jesus*

There is also the teaching from that passage in the Gospel in which Jesus, seeing the many people who by now were following him, asked his disciples: "How are we to buy bread, so that these people may eat?" (John 6:5). His disciples responded: "It is impossible. It would be better for you to send them away...." Instead, Jesus says to them: "No. You give them something to eat" (cf. Matt 14:16). He took the few loaves and fish that they had with them, and he blessed them, broke them, and distributed them to everyone. This is a very important lesson for us. It tells us that the little we have, if we entrust it to God's hands and share it with him in faith, becomes abundant wealth.

In his encyclical *Caritas in Veritate*, Benedict XVI affirms: "To feed the hungry is an ethical imperative for the universal Church.... The right to food, like the right to water, has an important place within the pursuit of other rights.... It is, therefore, necessary to cultivate a public conscience that considers food and access to water as universal rights of all human beings, without distinction or discrimination" (n. 27). Let us not forget the words of Jesus: "I am the bread of life" (John 6:35), and "If any one thirst, let him come to me" (John 7:37).

These words are a challenge for all believers, a challenge to recognize that our relationship with God—a God who has been revealed in Jesus, his merciful face—is connected to our giving food to the hungry and drink to the thirsty.

## The Large Crowd (6:34–44)[10]

We should note the verbs that describe God's intervention: he sees, hears, knows, comes down, and delivers. God does not remain indifferent. He is attentive and he acts.

In Jesus his Son, God has come down among us. He took flesh and showed his solidarity with humanity in all things but sin. Jesus identified with us: he became "the first-born among many brethren" (Rom 8:29). He was not content merely to teach the crowds but was concerned for their welfare, especially when he saw them hungry (cf. Mark 6:34–44) or without work (cf. Matt 20:3). He was concerned not only for men and women, but also for the fish of the sea, the birds of the air, plants and trees, all things great and small. He saw and embraced all creation. But he did more than just see; he touched people's lives. He spoke to them, helped them, and showed kindness to those in need. Not only this, but he felt strong emotions and he wept (cf. John 11:33–44). And he worked to put an end to suffering, sorrow, misery, and death.

## The Almond Tree (6:34–44)[11]

How beautiful were God's words to Jeremiah: "Jeremiah, what do you see?"

"A rod of almond, Lord."

"You have seen well, for I am watching over my word to perform it."

The flower of the almond tree is the first to blossom in spring. This is like the Lord who is there, watching over us, and he is always the first, like the almond tree, to love us. And we too will always have this surprise. When we draw near to God through works of charity, through prayer, in the Eucharist, in the word of God, we find that he is there, first, waiting for us; this is how he loves us. And just like the flower of the almond tree, he is the first. Truly, that verse from Jeremiah tells us so much.

A similar lesson can be gleaned from the scene presented in today's Gospel according to Mark, which says that "first, he had compassion for them, because they were like sheep without a shepherd" (v. 34). But today as well, there are so many confused people in our cities, in our countries—so many people.

When Jesus saw these confused people, he was moved. He began to teach them the doctrine, the matters of God, and the people heard him. They listened to him very closely because the Lord was good at speaking. He spoke to the heart.

Then Mark recounts that, realizing the five thousand people hadn't eaten, Jesus asked his disciples to see to it. And so Christ is first to go meet with the people. Perhaps on their part, the disciples got somewhat upset, felt annoyed, and their response was harsh: "Shall we go and buy two hundred denarii worth of bread and give it to them to eat?" Thus, God's love comes first; the disciples hadn't understood. But God's love is really like this: he is always waiting for us, he always surprises us. It is the Father, our Father who loves us so much, who is always ready to forgive us, always. And not once, but seventy times seven. Always! Indeed, he is a Father full of love. Therefore, in order to know this God who is love, we must climb the steps of love for our neighbor by works of charity, by the acts of mercy that our Lord taught us.

## Let Us Go Forth (6:37)[12]

Let us go forth, then, let us go forth to offer everyone the life of Jesus Christ. Here, I repeat for the entire Church what I have often said to the priests and laity of Buenos Aires: I prefer a Church that is bruised, hurting, and dirty because it has been out on the streets, rather than a Church that is unhealthy from being confined and from clinging to its own security. I do not want a Church concerned with being at the center and that then ends by being caught up in a web of obsessions and procedures. If something should rightly disturb us and trouble our consciences, it is the fact that so many of our brothers and sisters are living without the strength, light, and consolation born of friendship with Jesus Christ, without a community of faith to support them, without meaning and a goal in life. More than by fear of going astray, my hope is that we will be moved by the fear of remaining shut up within structures that give us a false sense of security, within rules that make us harsh judges, within habits that make us feel safe, while at our door people are starving and Jesus does not tire of saying to us: "Give them something to eat" (Mark 6:37).

## Solidarity (6:37)[13]

The Church has realized that the need to heed this plea [to feed the people] is itself born of the liberating action of grace within each of us, and thus it is not a question of a mission reserved only to a few: "The Church, guided by the Gospel of mercy and by love for mankind, hears the cry for justice and intends to respond to it with all her might."[14] In this context, we can understand Jesus's command to his disciples: "You yourselves give them something to eat!" (Mark 6:37): it means working to eliminate the structural causes of poverty and to promote the integral development of the poor, as well as small daily acts of solidarity in meeting the real needs that we encounter. The word "solidarity" is a little worn and at times poorly understood, but it refers to something more than a few sporadic acts of generosity. It presumes the creation of a new mindset that thinks in terms of community and the priority of the life of all over the appropriation of goods by a few.

## Hardened Hearts (6:45–52)[15]

In this passage, we see that the disciples did not understand about the loaves because their hearts were hardened. Yet, they were the apostles, the ones closest to Jesus. But they didn't understand. Even witnessing the miracle, even having seen that those people—more than five thousand—had eaten of five loaves, they didn't comprehend. Why? Because their hearts were hardened.

Many times in the Gospel, Jesus speaks of hardness of the heart. He rebukes the stiff-necked people and weeps over Jerusalem, which doesn't understand who he is. The Lord is faced with this hardness. It is such work for Jesus to make a heart more docile, to remove the hardness, and make it loving. And this work continues after the resurrection, with the disciples of Emmaus and many others.

How does a heart become hardened? How is it possible that the hearts of these people, who were always with Jesus, every day, who heard him, saw him . . . are hardened. How can a heart become like this? Yesterday, I asked my secretary: "How does a heart become hardened?" He helped me by indicating a series of circumstances that each person might face in his or her own personal experience.

First, the heart becomes hardened through *painful or harsh experiences*. This is the situation of those who have lived a very painful experience and don't want to begin another adventure. This is just what happened to the disciples at Emmaus after the resurrection. . . . This is a heart hardened by a painful experience. The same thing happened to Thomas: "No, no, I don't believe it. Unless I place my finger there, I won't believe it." The disciples' hearts were hard because they had suffered. There's a popular Argentine saying: "One who burns himself with milk will cry when he sees a cow." In other words, that painful experience keeps us from opening our heart.

Another reason the heart becomes hardened is that when *one becomes closed one makes a world within oneself*. . . . It is a closing off that can turn into many things, such as pride, self-sufficiency, thinking that I'm better than others, or even vanity. There are "mirror" men and women who are closed within themselves and watch themselves constantly; they could be called "religious narcissists." They have hard hearts because they are closed; they aren't open. And they try to protect themselves within the walls they build around themselves.

There is yet another reason that the heart becomes hardened: *insecurity*. It happens with those who think: "I don't feel secure and I am trying to hang on to something to be secure." This attitude is typical of people who really stick to the letter of the law. This happened with the Pharisees, with the Sadducees, and with the doctors of the law in the time of Jesus. They would have objected: "But the law says this, it says up to here," and [to make sure they would never even come close to that limit] they would create another commandment. In the end, the poor souls, they were leaning on three to four hundred commandments to feel secure.

In reality, all of them were secure people, but as a man or woman in a prison cell is secure behind the bars: it's a security without freedom. However, it is actually freedom that Jesus came to bring us. Saint Paul, for example, rebukes James and Peter because they do not accept the freedom that Jesus has brought us.

Hence the response to the initial question: "How does a heart become hardened?" The heart, when it hardens, is not free and if it isn't free it's *because it does not love*. This concept is expressed in the day's first reading (1 John 4:11–18), in which the apostle John speaks of "perfect love," which casts out fear. Indeed, there is no fear in love, but perfect love casts out fear, for fear has to do with punishment, and he who fears is not perfected in love. He isn't free. He always fears that something painful or sad might happen that could cause him to go the wrong way in life or to risk eternal salvation. Instead, this is only imagined, simply because that heart doesn't love. The disciples' hearts were hardened because they still hadn't learned how to love.

Thus, we can ask: Who teaches us how to love? Who frees us from this hardness? The Holy Spirit alone can do so. You can take a thousand courses in catechesis, a thousand courses in spirituality, a thousand courses in yoga, Zen, and all these things, but all of this will never be able to give you the freedom of the Son. Only the Holy Spirit moves your heart to say "Father"; he alone is capable of casting out, of breaking this hardness of the heart, of making it open to the Lord, open to the freedom of love. It is no coincidence that the disciples' hearts were hardened until the day of the ascension, when they said to the Lord: "Now the revolution will happen and the kingdom will come!" However, they didn't understand a thing. In reality, only when the Holy Spirit came did things change.

Therefore, let us ask the Lord for the grace to have a docile heart. May he save us from the slavery of a hardened heart and lead us to that beautiful freedom of perfect love, the freedom of the children of God, which the Holy Spirit alone can give.

## Working with God (6:53–56)[16]

Some medieval theologians explained that God, the Creator, first creates the universe, creates the heavens, the earth, and the living beings. This is the work of creation. However, creation is not the end. God continuously supports what he created, works to sustain what he created in order that it continue.

In this passage, we see "the other creation" of God, namely that of Jesus who comes to re-create what has been ruined by sin. And we see Jesus among the people. Indeed, Mark writes: "When they got out of the boat, people at once recognized him, and rushed about that whole region and began to bring the sick on mats to wherever they heard he was . . . all who touched [him] were healed" (vv. 54–56). This is the "re-creation," and the liturgy expresses the soul of the Church through this beautiful prayer: "O God, you created the universe so wondrously, but more wondrously you created redemption." Thus, this "second creation" is more wondrous than the first; this second work is more wondrous.

There is, then, the work of persevering in the faith, which Jesus says is done by the power of the Holy Spirit: "I will send the Paraclete and he will teach you and remind you, he will make you remember what I have said." It is the work of the Spirit within us, to keep the word of Jesus alive, to preserve creation, to guarantee that this creation does not die. The presence of the Spirit keeps the first and second creation alive.

In other words, God works. He continues to work and we can ask ourselves how we should respond to this creation of

God, which was born from love because God works through love. To the "first creation" we must respond with the responsibility the Lord gives us: "The earth is yours, foster it; make it grow!" For this reason, we have the responsibility to make the earth flourish, to make creation flourish, to safeguard it and make it flourish according to its laws. We are lords of creation, not masters. And we mustn't take control of creation but foster it and be faithful to its laws. Indeed, this is the first response to God's work: work to safeguard creation, to make it fruitful.

From this perspective, when we hear people hold meetings to consider how to safeguard creation, we could say: "They are 'green'!" But really, they aren't "green." This is Christian! And this is our response to God's "first creation." It is our responsibility! In fact, a Christian who doesn't safeguard creation, who doesn't make it flourish, is a Christian who isn't concerned with God's work, which is born of God's love for us. And this is the first response to the first creation: safeguard creation, make it flourish.

But, how do we respond to the "second creation"? Here, Paul the apostle gives us the right word, the true response: "Let yourselves reconcile with God." This is that open interior attitude for moving constantly on the path of inner reconciliation, of community reconciliation, because reconciliation is Christ's work. And Paul also says: "God has reconciled the world in Christ." Thus, to the "second creation" we say: "Yes, we must reconcile ourselves with the Lord."

And with regard to the work that the Holy Spirit does within us, of reminding us of Jesus's word, of explaining to us, of making us understand what Jesus said: How do we respond? It is again Paul who tells us not to grieve the Holy Spirit who is within us: Be attentive, he is your guest; he is within you; he works within you! Do not grieve the Holy Spirit (cf. Eph 4:30). And this is because we believe in a personal God. God is a person. He is the person of the Father, the person of the Son, the person of the Holy Spirit. After all, all three are engaged in this recreation, in this re-creation, in this perseverance in re-creation. Therefore, our response to all three is to safeguard creation and make it flourish, to reconcile ourselves with Jesus, with God in Jesus, in Christ, each day, and not to grieve the Holy Spirit, not to push him away. He is the guest in our heart, the One who accompanies us, who makes us grow.

# 7
# Clean and Unclean

## Two Identity Cards (7:1–13)[1]

Our true identity is found in the fact that we are created in the image, in the likeness of God (cf. Gen 1:20–2:4). But then, the question we could ask ourselves is: How can I know the image of God? How can I know what God is like in order to know what I'm like? Where can I find the image of God? The answer obviously cannot be found on a computer, or in an encyclopedia, or in books, because God's image is not in any catalog. There is only one way to find the image of God—my identity—and that is to journey. If we don't take up the journey, we will never know the face of God.

This desire for knowledge is also found in the Old Testament. The psalmist says many times: "I want to see your face," and even Moses asked this once of the Lord. But in reality, it isn't easy, because taking up the journey means letting go of many securities, many opinions about what God's image is like, and seeking it. In other words, it involves letting God and life put us to the test. It means taking a risk, for only then can we manage to know the face of God, the image of God, and take up the journey.

The prophets have done this. For instance, the great Elijah, after he wins and purifies the faith of Israel, hears the queen's threat and is afraid and doesn't know what to do. He takes up the journey. At a certain point, he would rather die, but God calls him, gives him food and drink, and says: "Keep going." This is how Elijah comes to the mountain where he finds God. His was thus a long journey, an arduous journey, a difficult journey, but it teaches us that those who don't take up the journey will never know the image of God; they will never find the face of God. It is a lesson for all of us: seated Christians, calm Christians will not know the face of God. They have the presumption to say: "God is like this, and like this. . . ." But in reality, they do not know God.

To journey we need to have that restlessness which God placed in our heart and which carries us onward to seek him. The same thing happened to Job who, with his trials, began to think: *What kind of God would let this happen to me?* His friends too, after days of great silence, began to talk and argue with him. But none of this was helpful. Through these arguments, Job did not come to know God. Instead, when he allowed himself to be questioned by the Lord in the trial, he met God. And from Job, we are also able to hear that word which will help us so much on this journey to find our identity: "I had heard of you with my ears, but now my eyes have seen you" (Job 42:5). And this is the heart of the matter; the encounter with God that can happen only by taking up the journey.

Of course, Job took up the journey cursing. He actually had the courage to curse his life and his history: "Let the day perish on which I was born . . ." (Job 3:3). In essence, sometimes on the journey of life we don't find the meaning of things. The prophet Jeremiah had the same experience. After being seduced by the Lord, he felt that curse: "Why me?" He wanted to remain calmly seated, but instead the Lord wanted to show him his face.

This applies to each of us. To know our identity, to know the image of God, we must take up the journey; we must be restless, not calm. This is precisely what it means to seek the face of God.

### *The Pharisees*

In this passage from Mark's Gospel, Jesus meets people who are afraid to take up the journey and who create a "caricature" of God. But that is a false identity, because these non-restless ones have calmed the restlessness of their heart by describing God with commandments. In doing so, however, they have forgotten God and see only the tradition of men. And when they experience uncertainty, they invent or make up another commandment. Jesus says to the scribes and Pharisees who accumulate commandments: "You are making void the word of God through your tradition which you hand on. And many such things you do." This is the false identity that we might have if we do not take up the journey, if we remain calm, without restlessness of heart.

The Lord praises them but reprimands them where it hurts the most. He praises them: "You have a fine way of rejecting the commandment of God, in order to keep your tradition." But then he reprimands them with regard to the most powerful point of the commandments having to do with one's neighbor. In fact, Jesus recalls that Moses said: "Honor your father and your mother" and "Whoever speaks evil of father or mother must surely die." But, Jesus says to them, "You say that if anyone tells father or mother, 'Whatever support you might have had from me is Corban' (that is, an offering to God)—then you no longer permit doing anything for a father or mother" (vv. 10–12). In doing so, in abiding by the mildest commandment, they wash their hands of the strongest one, the only one with a promise of blessing. And so, they are at peace, they are calm, they do not take up the journey. This then, is the image of God that they have. In reality, their "journey" is one that doesn't move; it is a still journey. They deny their parents, but fulfill the laws of the tradition they have made.

### *A comparison*

Here are two types of identity. The first is the one we all have because the Lord made us like this; it is the one that tells us: take up the journey and you will know your identity, for you are the image of God, you were created in the likeness of God. Take up the journey and look for God. The other, however, reassures us: "No, relax. Fulfill all these commandments and this is God. This is the face of God." We ask the Lord to give everyone the grace of courage to always take up the journey, to seek the Lord's face, that face which we will see one day, but which we must look for here on Earth.

## The Spirit of the Law (7:1–8, 14–15, 21–23)[2]

In today's passage, Jesus addresses an important topic for all believers: the authenticity of our obedience to the word of God against any worldly contamination or legalistic formalism. The narrative opens with the objection that the scribes and Pharisees address to Jesus, accusing his disciples of failing to observe the ritual precepts according to tradition. In this way, those challenging him try to strike at Jesus's reliability and authority as teacher when they accuse his disciples of not living according to the tradition of the elders (v. 5). But Jesus responds emphatically, saying: "Isaiah prophesied rightly about you hypocrites, as it is written, 'This people honors me with their lips, but their hearts are far from me; in vain do they worship me, teaching human precepts as doctrine'" (vv. 6–7). These are clear and emphatic words! "Hypocrite" is, so to speak, one of the strongest adjectives that Jesus uses in the Gospel, and he uses it as he addresses the teachers of religion—doctors of the law, scribes, and so on.

Indeed, Jesus wants to rouse the scribes and Pharisees from the error they have fallen into. And what is this error? That of distorting God's will, neglecting his commandments in order to observe human traditions. Jesus's reaction is severe because something great is at stake. It concerns the truth of the relationship between human beings and God, the authenticity of religious life. A hypocrite is a liar; such a person is not authentic.

Today, too, the Lord invites us to avoid the danger of giving more importance to form than to substance. He calls us to recognize, ever anew, what is the true core of the experience of faith—that is, love of God and love of neighbor—by purifying it of the hypocrisy of legalism and ritualism.

Today's gospel message is also reinforced by the voice of the apostle James, who tells us, in brief, the true meaning of religion: pure religion is "to care for orphans and widows in their distress, and to keep oneself unstained by the world" (Jas 1:27). "To care for orphans and widows" is to practice charity toward neighbors, beginning with the neediest, frailest, and most marginalized people. They are the people whom God takes care of in a special way, and he asks us to do the same.

"To keep oneself unstained by the world" does not mean to isolate oneself and close oneself off from reality. No. Here, too, there must be not an exterior attitude but one that is interior, substantive. It means being vigilant so that our way of thinking and acting may not be polluted by worldliness, vanity, greed, or arrogance. Actually, a man or woman who lives in vanity, in greed, or in arrogance and at the same time believes and shows himself or herself as being religious and even goes so far as to condemn others is a hypocrite.

Let us make an examination of conscience to see how we embrace the word of God. On Sunday we listen to it at Mass. If we listen to it in a distracted or superficial way, it will not be of much use. Instead, we must welcome the word with open minds and hearts, as good soil, in such a way that it may be assimilated and bear fruit in real life. Jesus says that the word of God is like wheat; it is a seed that must grow in practical deeds. In this way, the Word itself purifies our heart and actions, so that our relationship with God and with others is freed from hypocrisy.

## Honor Your Father and Mother (7:8–13)[3]

First, let us think of our parents. Jesus told the Pharisees that abandoning one's parents is contrary to God's law (cf. Mark 7:8–13). We do well to remember that each of us is a son or daughter. Even if one becomes an adult, or an elderly person, even if one becomes a parent, if one occupies a position of responsibility, underneath all of this one still has the identity of a child. We are all sons and daughters. And this always brings us back to the fact that we did not give ourselves life but that we received it. The great gift of life is the first gift that we received.

Hence, the fourth commandment asks children . . . to honor their father and mother (cf. Exod 20:12). This commandment comes immediately after those dealing with God himself. Indeed, it has to do with something sacred, something divine, something at the basis of every other kind of human respect. The biblical formulation of the fourth commandment goes on to say: "that your days may be long in the land which the Lord your God gives you." The virtuous bond between generations is the guarantee of the future, the guarantee of a truly humane society. A society with children who do not honor their parents is a society without honor. . . . It is a society destined to be filled with surly and greedy young people.

There is, however, another side to the coin. As the word of God tells us, "a man leaves his father and his mother" (Gen 2:24). This does not always happen, and a marriage is hampered by the failure to make this necessary sacrifice and surrender. Parents must not be abandoned or ignored, but marriage itself demands that they be "left," so that the new home will be a true hearth, a place of security, hope, and future plans, and the couple can truly become "one flesh." In some marriages, one spouse keeps secrets from the other, confiding them instead to his or her parents. Consequently, the opinions of their parents become more important than the feelings and opinions of their spouse. This situation cannot go on for long, and even if it takes time, both spouses need to make the effort to grow in trust and communication. Marriage challenges husbands and wives to find new ways of being sons and daughters.

### Purities and Impurities (7:15, 21–22)[4]

In the Gospel, we see Jesus reject a certain conception of ritual purity bound to exterior practices, one that forbade all contact with things and people—including lepers and strangers—considered impure. To the Pharisees who, like so many Jews of their time, ate nothing without first performing ritual ablutions and observing the many traditions associated with cleansing vessels, Jesus responds categorically: "There is nothing outside a man which by going into him can defile him; but the things which come out of a man are what defile him. For from within, out of the heart of man, come evil thoughts, fornication, theft, murder, adultery, coveting, wickedness, deceit, licentiousness, envy, slander, pride, foolishness" (Mark 7:15, 21–22).

### The Human Heart (7:14–23)[5]

The good that humanity accomplishes is not the result of calculations or policies, nor is it the result of hereditary genetics or of social status. Rather, it is the fruit of a willing heart, of free choice that seeks true goodness. Science and technology are not enough; doing good works requires wisdom of heart.

In various ways, sacred scripture tells us that good or evil intentions do not enter the person from without, but come from within one's heart. "From within," Jesus said, "out of the heart of man, come evil thoughts" (Mark 7:21). In the Bible, the heart is the organ not only of feelings but also of spiritual faculties, reason, and will; it is the seat of decisions, and of the manner of thinking and acting. The wisdom of choice, open to the prompting of the Holy Spirit, also concerns the heart. From here are born good works but also mistakes when the truth and the prompting of the Spirit are rejected. The heart, in other words, is the synthesis of humanity formed by the very hands of God (cf. Gen 2:7) and beheld by its Creator with singular satisfaction (cf. Gen 1:31). God pours his own wisdom into the heart of man. . . .

When the heart moves away from goodness and from the truth contained in the word of God, it is exposed to a multitude of dangers. It is deprived of direction and risks calling good evil and evil good. Virtue is lost, easily replaced by sin and then by vice. Those who step onto this slippery slope fall into moral error and are burdened with an increasing sense of existential anguish.

Scripture shows us the dynamic of a hardened heart: the more the heart leans toward selfishness and evil, the harder it is to change. Jesus says: "Everyone who commits sin is a slave to sin" (John 8:34). When the heart is corrupted, the consequences in social life are grave, as the prophet Jeremiah reminds us: "You have eyes and heart only for your dishonest gain, for shedding innocent blood, and for practicing oppression and violence" (22:17).

## The Good News (7:22)[6]

Jesus himself lived in violent times, yet he taught that the true battlefield, where violence and peace meet, is the human heart: for "it is from within, from the human heart, that evil intentions come" (Mark 7:21). But Christ's message here offers a radically positive approach. He unfailingly preached God's unconditional love, which welcomes and forgives. He taught his disciples to love their enemies (cf. Matt 5:44) and to turn the other cheek (cf. Matt 5:39). When he stopped her accusers from stoning the woman caught in adultery (cf. John 8:1–11), and when, on the night before he died, he told Peter to put away his sword (cf. Matt 26:52), Jesus marked out the path of nonviolence. He walked that path to the very end, to the cross; he became our peace and put an end to hostility (cf. Eph 2:14–16). Whoever accepts the Good News of Jesus is able to acknowledge the violence within and be healed by God's mercy, becoming in turn an instrument of reconciliation. In the words of Saint Francis of Assisi: "As you announce peace with your mouth, make sure that you have greater peace in your hearts."[7]

## Two Paths (7:24–30)[8]

The First Book of Kings speaks about Solomon (11:4–13), and the Gospel of Mark (7:24–30) presents the image of the woman "who spoke Greek and was Syro-Phoenician" and who begged Jesus to drive out the demon from her daughter. Solomon and the woman take two opposite paths. Today, the Church invites us to reflect on the journey from paganism and idolatry to the living God, and also on the journey from the living God to idolatry.

In turning to Jesus for help, the woman is brave, like any desperate mother who would do anything for the health of her child. She had been told that there was a good man, a prophet, and so she decided to go and look for Jesus, even though she did not believe in the God of Israel. For the sake of her daughter, she was not ashamed of how she might look before the apostles, who might say among themselves: "What is this pagan doing here?" She approached Jesus to beg him to help her daughter who was possessed by an unclean spirit. But Jesus responded to her request by saying, "I came first for the sheep of the house of Israel." Then he continues to speak with harsh words, saying: "Let the children help themselves first, because it is not good to take the children's bread and throw it to the dogs."

The woman—who certainly had never attended university—did not respond to Jesus with worldly wisdom, but instead with a mother's courageous heart, with love. She said: "Even the dogs under the table will eat the children's crumbs," as if to say: "Give me the crumbs!" Moved by her faith, the Lord worked a miracle. She returned home, found her daughter lying on her bed, and the demon was gone.

Essentially, it is the story of a mother who risked making a fool of herself, but still persisted out of love for her daughter. She left paganism and idolatry, and found for her daughter health and for herself the living God. Hers was the way of a person of good will, one who seeks God and finds him. For her faith, the Lord blessed her. This is also the story of so many people who still make this journey. The Lord waits for these people who are moved by the Holy Spirit. There are people who make this journey every day in the Church of God, silently seeking the Lord because they let themselves be carried forward by the Holy Spirit.

### *The opposite path*

However, there is also the opposite path, which is represented by the figure of Solomon. He was the wisest man on earth, and he had received many great blessings; he had inherited a united country, consolidated by his father, David. King Solomon had universal fame; he had complete power. He was also a believer in God. So why did he lose his faith? The answer lies in the biblical passage: "His women made him divert his heart to follow other gods, and his heart did not remain with the Lord, his God, as the heart of David his father did."

Solomon liked women. He had many concubines and would travel with them here and there, each with her own god, her own idol. These women slowly weakened Solomon's heart. He therefore lost the integrity of the faith. When one woman asked him for a small temple for her god, he built it on a mountain. And when another woman asked him for incense to burn for an idol, he bought it. In doing so, his heart was weakened and he lost his faith.

The wisest man in the world lost his faith as a result of allowing himself to become corrupt because of an indiscreet love, a love without discretion, and because of his passions. Yet, you might say: "But Father, Solomon did not lose his faith. He still believed in God. He could recite the Bible from memory." To have faith does not mean being able to recite the Creed: you can still recite the Creed after having lost your faith!

Solomon, like his father, David, sinned. But then Solomon continued living as a sinner and became corrupt: his heart was corrupted by idolatry. His father, David, was a sinner, but the Lord had forgiven all of his sins because David was humble and asked for forgiveness. Instead, Solomon's vanity and passions led him to corruption. The heart is precisely the place where one can lose one's faith.

The king, therefore, takes the opposite path from that of the Syro-Phoenician woman: she leaves the idolatry of paganism and comes to find the living God, while Solomon leaves the living God and finds idolatry. What a poor man! She was a sinner, sure, just as we all are. But he was corrupt.

### *The word of God*

It was the seed of evil passions growing in Solomon's heart that led him to idolatry. To prevent this seed from developing, we must receive with meekness the word that has been planted in us and can lead us to salvation. Knowing this, we follow the path of the Canaanite woman, the pagan woman, accepting the word of God that has been planted in us and will lead us to salvation. The word of God is powerful, and it will safeguard us on the path and prevent us from the destructive power of corruption and all that leads to idolatry.

## The Journey to Faith (7:31–37)[9]

The Gospel today recounts Jesus's healing of a man who was deaf and had a speech impediment, an incredible event that shows how Jesus reestablishes the full communication of man with God and with other people. The miracle is set in the region of the Decapolis, that is, in a completely pagan territory. Thus, this deaf man who is brought before Jesus becomes the symbol of the unbeliever who completes a journey to faith. In effect, his deafness expresses the inability to hear and to understand, not just the words of other, but also the word of God. And Saint Paul reminds us that "faith comes from what is heard" (Rom 10:17).

The first thing that Jesus does is to take this man *far from the crowd*: He doesn't want to publicize this deed he intends to carry out, but he also doesn't want his word to be lost in the din of voices and the chatter of those around. The word of God that Christ brings us needs silence to be welcomed as the word that heals, that reconciles, and that reestablishes communication.

Then we are told about two gestures that Jesus makes. He touches the ears and the tongue of the deaf man. To reestablish a relationship with this man whose communication is impeded, he first seeks to reestablish contact. But the miracle is a gift that comes from on high, a gift that Jesus implores from the Father. That's why *he raises his eyes to the heavens and orders, "Be opened."* And the ears of the deaf man are opened, the knot of his tongue is untied, and he begins to speak correctly (cf. v. 35).

The lesson we can take from this scene is that God is not closed in on himself; instead, *he opens himself and places himself in communication* with humanity. In his immense mercy, he overcomes the abyss of the infinite difference between him and us, and he comes to meet us. To bring about this communication, God becomes man. It is not enough for him to speak to us through the law and the prophets, but instead he makes himself present in the person of his Son, the Word made flesh. Jesus is the great "bridge-builder" who builds in himself the great bridge of full communion with the Father.

But this Gospel speaks to us also about ourselves. Often we are drawn up and closed in on ourselves, and we create many inaccessible and inhospitable islands. Even the most basic human relationships can sometimes create spaces incapable of reciprocal openness. And we all know of the closed couple, the closed family, the closed group, the closed parish, the closed country. And this is not from God! This is from us. This is our sin.

However, at the beginning of our Christian life, at baptism, it is precisely this gesture and word of Jesus that are present: "*Ephphatha*!"—"Be opened!" And behold the miracle has been worked. We are healed of the deafness of selfishness and the impediment of being closed in on ourselves, and of sin, and we have been inserted into the great family of the Church. We can hear God who speaks to us and communicates his word to those who have never before heard it, or to those who have forgotten it and buried it in the thorns of the anxieties and the traps of the world.

8

# The Mission and the Cross

## Three Gestures (8:1–9)[1]

We have come from a variety of places, areas, and towns to celebrate the living presence of God among us. We have traveled from our homes and communities to be together as God's holy people. The cross and the mission image remind us of all those communities that were born of the name of Jesus in these lands. We are their heirs.

The Gospel speaks of a situation much like our own. Like those four thousand people who gathered to hear Jesus, we too want to listen to his words and to receive his life. Like them, we are in the presence of the Master, the Bread of Life.

### *From generation to generation*

I am moved when I see many mothers carrying their children on their shoulders—like so many of you here! Carrying them, you bring your lives and the future of your people. You bring all your joys and hopes. You bring the blessing of the earth and all its fruits. You bring the work of your hands, hands that work today in order to weave tomorrow's hopes and dreams. But those people's shoulders were also weighed down by bitter disappointments and sorrows, scarred by experiences of injustice and of justice denied. They bore on their shoulders all the joy and pain of their land. You too bear the memory of your own people. Because every people has a memory, a memory that is passed on from generation to generation, all peoples have a memory which continues to move forward.

### *Keeping hope alive*

We so often tire of this journey. We so often lack the strength to keep hope alive. How often have we experienced situations that dull our memory, weaken our hope, and make us lose our reason for rejoicing? And then a kind of sadness takes over. We think only of ourselves; we forget that we are a people that is loved, a chosen people. And the loss of that memory disorients us; it closes our hearts to others, and especially to the poor.

### *The temptation to despair*

We may feel the way the disciples did when they saw those crowds of people gathered there. They begged Jesus to send them away—"to send them home"—since it was impossible to provide food for so many people. Faced with so many kinds of hunger in our world, we can say to ourselves: "Sorry, but things don't add up; we will never manage, there is nothing to be done." And so our hearts yield to despair.

A despairing heart finds it easy to succumb to a way of thinking that is becoming ever more widespread in our world today. It is a mentality in which everything has a price, everything can be bought, and everything is negotiable. This way of thinking has room for only a select few, while it discards all those who are "unproductive," unsuitable, or unworthy, since clearly those people don't "add up."

Jesus again turns to us and says: "No, no, they don't need to be excluded, they don't need to go away; you yourselves, give them something to eat."

These words of Jesus are particularly relevant for us today: No one needs to be excluded, no one has to be discarded; you yourselves, give them something to eat.... Jesus's way of seeing things leaves no room for the mentality that would cut bait on the weak and those most in need. Taking the lead, setting an example, he shows us the way forward. What he does can be summed up in three words. He *takes* a little bread and some fish, he *blesses* them, and then he *gives* them to his disciples to share with the crowd. And this is how the miracle takes place. It is not magic or sorcery. With these three gestures, Jesus is able to turn a mentality that discards others into a mindset of communion, a mindset of community. I would like briefly to look at each of these actions.

### *Taking*

This is the starting point. Jesus takes his own and their lives very seriously. He looks them in the eye, and he knows what they are experiencing, what they are feeling. He sees in their eyes all that is present in the memory and the hearts of his people.... He thinks of all the good that they can do, all the good upon which they can build. He is not concerned with material objects, cultural treasures, or lofty ideas. He is concerned with people. The greatest wealth of a society is measured by the lives of its people; it is gauged by its elderly, who pass on their knowledge and the memory of their people to the young. Jesus never detracts from the dignity of anyone, no matter how little they possess or seem capable of contributing. He takes everything as it comes.

### *Blessing*

Jesus takes what he is given and blesses his heavenly Father. He knows that everything is God's gift, so he treats things not as "objects" but as part of a life that is the fruit of God's merciful love. He values them. He goes beyond mere appearances, and in this gesture of blessing and praise, he asks the Father for the gift of the Holy Spirit. Blessing has this double aspect: thanksgiving and transformation. It is a recognition that life is always a gift that, when placed in the hands of God, starts to multiply. Our Father never abandons us; he makes everything multiply.

### *Giving*

With Jesus, there can be no *taking* that is not a *blessing*, and no *blessing* that is not also a *giving*. Blessing is always mission; its purpose is to share what we ourselves have received. For it is only in giving, in sharing, that we find the source of our joy and come to experience salvation. Giving makes it possible to refresh the memory of God's holy people, who are invited to be and to bring the joy of salvation to others. The hands that Jesus lifts to bless God in heaven are the same hands that gave bread to the hungry crowd. We can imagine now how those people passed the loaves of bread and the fish from hand to hand, until they came to those farthest away. Jesus generated a current among his followers as they shared what they had, made it a gift for others, and so ate their fill. Unbelievably, there were even leftovers—enough to fill seven baskets. A memory that is taken, a memory that is blessed, and a memory that is given always satisfies people's hunger.

### *The Eucharist*

The Eucharist is the "bread broken for the life of the world." That is the theme of the Fifth Eucharistic Congress to be held in Tarija, which today we inaugurate. The Eucharist is a sacrament of communion that draws us out of our individualism in order to live together as disciples. It gives us the certainty that all that we have, all that we are, if it is taken, blessed, and given, can, by God's power, by the power of his love, become the bread of life for all.

And the Church celebrates the Eucharist. She celebrates the memory of the Lord, the sacrifice of the Lord, because the Church is a community of remembrance. In fidelity to the Lord's command, she never ceases to say: "Do this in remembrance of me" (Luke 22:19). Generation after generation, throughout the world, she celebrates the mystery of the Bread of Life. She makes it present, truly real, and she gives it to us. Jesus asks us to share in his life, and through us he allows this gift to multiply in our world. We are not isolated individuals, separated from one another, but rather a people of remembrance, a remembrance ever renewed and ever shared with others.

### *The logic of love*

A life of remembrance needs others. It demands exchange, encounter, and a genuine solidarity capable of entering into the mindset of taking, blessing, and giving. It demands the logic of love.

Mary, like many of you, bore in her heart the memory of her people. She pondered the life of her Son. She personally experienced God's grandeur and joyfully proclaimed that he "fills the hungry with good things" (Luke 1:53). Today, may she be our model. Like her, let us trust in the goodness of the Lord, who does great things with smallness, with the lowliness of his servants.

## Holy Patience (8:11–13)[2]

What James the apostle tells us seems strange: "Consider it pure joy, my brothers, when you face trials of all kinds," (Jas 1:1–11). Can undergoing a trial bring us joy? James continues: "Know that your faith, with many trials, produces patience. And patience will have its full effect, that you may be perfect and complete, lacking nothing." Here, the apostle is suggesting that we bring life into this rhythm of patience.

Patience, however, is not resignation, it is something quite different. Patience means bearing the things of life, the things that are not good, the bad things, the things that we do not want. Such patience will help our lives to mature. Those who have no patience instead want everything at once, all in a hurry. Those who do not know the wisdom of patience are whimsical, and they end up behaving like impetuous children who say: "I want this, I want that, I do not like this," and are never satisfied.

### *Temptations*

In responding to the Pharisees in the Gospel of Mark, the Lord asks: "Why does this generation seek a sign?" In other words, he is saying that this generation is like children who do not dance when they hear joyful music and do not cry when they hear a dirge. Nothing is right! In fact, the person who has no patience is a person who will not grow, who remains stuck in childish whims, not knowing how to take life as it comes, and who can say only "either this or nothing!"

When there is no patience, there is the temptation to become capricious like children. Another temptation of those without patience is omnipotence, which causes one to say: "I want things right away!" The Lord is referring precisely to this when the Pharisees ask him for "a sign from heaven." What do they want? They want a show, a miracle. Ultimately, it is the same temptation that the devil offers Jesus in the desert, asking him to do something—or to show his power by throwing himself from the temple.

### *The music of patience*

In asking Jesus for a sign, however, the Pharisees confuse God's way of acting with the way of a sorcerer. God does not act like a sorcerer. God has his way of going forward: his patience. Every time we go to the sacrament of reconciliation we sing a hymn to God's patience. The Lord, with great patience, carries us on his shoulders!

The Christian life has to be carried out with this music of patience, because it was the music of our fathers: the people of God, the music of those who believed in the word of God, who followed the commandment that the Lord gave to our father Abraham: "Walk before me and be blameless."

The people of God suffered greatly: they were persecuted, murdered, and had to hide in caverns and in caves (cf. Hebrews 11). They had joy, the happiness to welcome the promises from afar. It is precisely this patience that we must have amid trials. The patience of an adult and the patience of God that leads us, that carries us on his shoulders, and the patience of our people. How patient our people are even now!

There are many suffering people who are able to live their lives with patience. They do not ask for a sign; instead, they know how to read the signs of the times. They know that when figs grow on a tree, it is springtime. The impatient people presented in the Gospel wanted a sign but did not know how to read the signs of the times. For this reason they did not recognize Jesus.

### *Everyday sanctity*

The Letter to the Hebrews states clearly that the world was unworthy of God's people. But today, we can say the same about those of our people who suffer, who suffer many, many things, but do not lose the smile of faith, which has the joy of faith. Indeed, the world is not worthy of any of them. These are the people—our people—in our parishes and institutions, who carry the Church forward with their everyday sanctity.

## Resist Temptation (8:14–21)[3]

Every person is tempted by his or her own passions, which attract and seduce. Then the passions conceive and create sin, and once that sin is committed, it brings forth death.

But where does temptation come from? How does it act within us? The apostle James tells us that sin does not come from God but from our passions, from our inner weaknesses, from the wounds that original sin has left within us. From there comes temptation.

Initially, temptation begins in a soothing way, but then it grows. Jesus himself spoke of this when he told the parable of the seeds and the weeds (cf. Matt 13:24–30). The seeds grew, but the weeds planted by the enemy also grew.... If one does not stop them, then they occupy everything, and that is when infection occurs. Temptation grows and it hates solitude; it will try to spread to another to have company. This is how it accumulates people, spreading to others. Finally there is justification; we justify ourselves in order to feel fine with ourselves....

This is what happened to the apostles who were in the boat: they had forgotten to bring bread and began to blame each other and discuss who had made the mistake of forgetting it. Jesus looked at them. I think that he smiled as he watched them. And he said to them: "Do you remember the yeast of the Pharisees and Herod? Take heed, beware!" Yet they did not understand anything, because they were so caught up in blame that they did not have room for anything else; they did not have light to understand the word of God.

The same happens when we fall into temptation. We do not hear the word of God and we do not understand. Jesus had to remind the apostles of the multiplication of the loaves to help them to get out of the mindset that they were in. This happens because temptation closes every horizon and in this way leads us to sin. When we are being tempted, only the word of God, the word of Jesus, can save us. Listening to his word opens horizons because he is always ready to help us escape from temptation. Jesus is great because he not only helps us to get out of temptation, he also gives us more faith.

### *Look to the horizon*

Recall the conversation between Jesus and Peter (cf. Luke 22:31–32), in which the Lord tells Peter that the devil wants to sift him like wheat. At the same time, Jesus tells him that he has prayed for him and gives him a new mission: "When once you have turned back, strengthen your brothers." Therefore, Jesus not only expects to help us escape temptation but he also trusts us. This is a source of great strength, because he always opens up new horizons while, through temptation, the devil tries to close us in and create situations that cause us to fight and seek justification for accusing others.

Let us not be ensnared by temptation. We can escape temptation only by listening to the word of Jesus. Let us ask the Lord to always say to us in times of temptation, as he did so patiently with the disciples: "Stop. Do not worry. Lift up your eyes. Look to the horizon. Do not close yourself in. Move forward." In moments of temptation, his word will save us from falling into sin.

## Our Capacity to Destroy and Build (8:14–21)[4]

The passage from the Book of Genesis (6:5–8; 7:1–5, 10) makes us think about our capacity for destruction. We are capable of destroying everything that God made when we think we are more powerful than God. Thus, God can make good things, but man is capable of destroying them.

Even starting from the beginning, in the first chapters of the Bible, we find many examples. For example, man summons the flood through his wickedness; he summons the fire out of heaven, to Sodom and Gomorrah, out of his wickedness; he creates confusion, the division of humanity—the Tower of Babel—with his wickedness. In other words, humans are capable of destruction; we are all capable of destruction. This is confirmed again in Genesis with a very, very sharp phrase: "The wickedness of humankind was great in the earth, and every inclination of the thoughts of their hearts was only evil continually" (Gen 6:5).

It isn't a question of being too negative, because this is the truth. At this point, we are even capable of destroying fraternity, as demonstrated in the story of Cain and Abel found in the first pages of the Bible. This scene is the beginning of wars: jealousy, envy, greed for power, to have more power. Yes, this seems negative, but it is realistic. After all, one need only pick up a newspaper to see that more than 90 percent of the news is about destruction. And we see this every day!

### *The fundamental question*

What happens in the heart of man? Jesus once warned his disciples that evil does not enter a man's heart because he eats something that isn't pure, but rather, it comes out of the heart. And all wickedness comes out of the heart of humankind. Indeed, our weak heart is wounded. There is always that desire for autonomy which leads one to say: "I do what I want, and if I want to do this, I do it! And if I want to make war over this, I do it! And if I want to destroy my family over this, I do it! And if I want to kill my neighbor over this, I do it." This is what we hear every day on the news, observing that newspapers don't tell us about the lives of saints.

Therefore, returning to the central question: Why are we like this? Because we have the opportunity to destroy. This is the problem! And in doing so—with war, with arms trafficking—we are entrepreneurs of death! There are countries that sell arms to this one that is at war with that one, and they also sell them to that one, so that the war continues. The problem is precisely the capacity for destruction that comes not from our neighbor but from us!

Every innermost intent of the heart is nothing but evil. We have this seed inside, this possibility. But we also have the Holy Spirit who saves us. It is thus a matter of choosing to start with the little things. And so, a woman goes to the market and finds someone else, starts to gossip, to speak ill of her neighbor, about that woman over there: this woman kills, this woman is evil. And this happens at the market but also in the parish, in associations, when there is jealousy. The envious ones go to the priest to say, "This one no, this one yes, this one does. . . ." And this, too, is evil—the capacity to destroy—which all of us have.

In this gospel passage, Jesus lightly reprimands the disciples who have been arguing: "You were supposed to bring the bread—no, you were!" Basically, the Twelve, as usual, were arguing among themselves. And Jesus says something beautiful to them: "Take heed, beware of the leaven of the Pharisees and the leaven of Herod." He simply makes an example of two people: Herod is bad, he is an assassin, and the Pharisees are hypocrites. The Lord also speaks of "leaven," but the disciples do not understand.

The fact is that the disciples were speaking about bread, about this bread, and Jesus tells them that "leaven is dangerous; what we have inside is what leads us to destroy. Take heed, beware!" Then Jesus says: "Are your hearts hardened? Do you not remember when I broke the five loaves, the door of God's salvation? In fact, nothing good ever comes from arguing." Then he added, "There will always be division, destruction!" He continued: "Think about salvation, about what God did for us, and make the right choice!" But the disciples did not understand because their hearts were hardened by passion, by the wickedness of arguing among themselves to see who was to blame for forgetting the bread.

We should take this message of the Lord seriously because this isn't something strange, this isn't a Martian talking. No! These are things that happen in everyday life. And to confirm this, we only need to pick up the newspaper, nothing more!

However, we are capable of doing much good. Consider Mother Teresa, for example, a woman of our era. If all of us are capable of doing such good, we are also capable of destroying in great and small measure, within a family—of destroying the children, not letting them grow freely, not helping them to grow well, and thus in some way, nullifying the children. We have this capacity and this is the reason constant meditation, prayer, and discussion among ourselves is necessary, to avoid falling into this wickedness which destroys everything.

We have the strength to do it, as Jesus reminds us. Today he tells us: "Remember. Remember me, who spilled my blood for you; remember me, who saved you, who saves everyone; remember me, who has the power to accompany you on the journey of life, not on the road of evil, but on the path of goodness, of doing good for others; not on the path of destruction, but on the path of building: building a family, building a city, building a culture, building a homeland, always more!"

## The Messianic Secret (8:27–33)[5]

Peter was certainly the most courageous one that day, when Jesus asked his disciples: "But who do you say that I am?" Peter responded decisively: "You are the Christ." Peter was likely quite satisfied within himself, thinking, *I answered well!* And truly, he had answered well.

However, his dialogue with Jesus did not end so well. The Lord began to explain what would happen, but Peter did not like what he was hearing. He did not like the path that Jesus set forth.

Today, too, we hear many times within ourselves the same question that Jesus addressed to the apostles. Jesus turns to us and asks us: "Who am I for you?" Who is Jesus Christ for each of us, for me? Who is Jesus Christ? Surely, we will respond as Peter did, and as we learned in the catechism: "You are the Son of the living God, you are the Redeemer, you are the Lord!"

### *Peter's reaction*

Peter's reaction was different once Jesus began to explain all that would happen to him: the Son of man would have to suffer many things, and be rejected by the elders and by the chief priests and the scribes, and be killed, and after three days rise again. Peter most certainly did not like this talk. He thought: "You are the Christ! Conquer and let's move ahead!" Peter did not understand the path of suffering that Jesus was talking about. So much so, the Gospel tells us, that Peter took him, and began to reproach him. He was so pleased with having responded, "You are the Christ," that he felt he had the strength to reproach Jesus.

The Gospel tells us that Jesus "turning and seeing his disciples, he rebuked Peter, and said, 'Get behind me, Satan! For you are not on the side of God, but of men.'"

Therefore, in order to respond to that question which we all hear in our hearts—Who is Jesus for us?—what we have learned and studied in the catechism does not suffice. Certainly, it is important to study and to know it, but that is not enough. To know him truly, we need to travel the path that Peter traveled. Indeed, after this humiliation, Peter continued on with Jesus. He saw the miracles that Jesus worked and saw his power. Then he paid the taxes, as Jesus had told him; he caught the fish and took the coin from its mouth. He saw so many miracles of this kind!

However, at a certain point, Peter denied Jesus. He betrayed him. That is when he learned the difficult science—

which is more wisdom than science—of tears, of weeping. Peter asked for forgiveness from the Lord.

And yet, in the uncertainty of Easter morning, Peter did not know what to think about all that the women had told him concerning the empty tomb. And so he went to the tomb. The Gospel does not recount that moment explicitly, but it does say that the Lord met Peter and that Peter encountered the living Lord, alone, face-to-face.

In the course of the forty days following the Lord's resurrection, Peter heard many explanations from Jesus about the kingdom of God. And he may have been tempted to think: *Ah, now I know who Jesus Christ is!* However, he still lacked so much in terms of knowing who Jesus is.

And so, that morning, on the shore of Tiberias, Peter was questioned once again. Three times. And he felt ashamed as he remembered the evening of Holy Thursday—the three times he had denied Jesus. He remembered weeping. On the shore of Tiberias Peter did not weep bitterly as on Holy Thursday, but he did weep. I am sure that Peter wept as he spoke those moving words: "You know everything, Lord, you know that I love you."

### *The disciple's path*

Therefore, one understands the question posed to Peter—"Who am I for you?"—only within the context of a long journey, after having traveled a long path, a path of grace and of sin. It is the disciple's path. In fact, following Jesus enables us to know Jesus. We must follow Jesus through our virtues and also through our sins. Always following Jesus!

In order to know Jesus, what is needed is not a study of notions but rather life as a disciple, for in journeying with Jesus we learn who he is... we come to know Jesus as disciples. We come to know him in the daily encounter with the Lord, through our victories and through our weaknesses. It is precisely through these encounters that we draw close to him and come to know him more deeply, for it is in these everyday encounters that we acquire what Saint Paul calls the mind of Christ, the hermeneutic for judging all things.

It is a journey that we cannot make alone. In Matthew's account (16:13–28), Jesus says to Peter: "The confession that I am the Son of God, the Messiah, you have not learned from human knowledge; it has been revealed to you by my Father." And Jesus will go on to say to his disciples: "The Holy Spirit, whom I shall send to you, will teach you all things and will make you understand all that I have taught you."

Therefore, we come to know Jesus as disciples on the path of life, following behind him. But this is not enough. In reality, this is a work of the Holy Spirit, who is a great worker. He is not a union organizer; he is a great worker. He is always at work in us, and he carries out the great work of explaining the mystery of Jesus and of giving us the mind of Christ.

Let us ask the Father to grant us a deeper knowledge of Christ, and let us ask the Holy Spirit to explain to us this mystery.

## The Logic of the Cross (8:33)[6]

Following and accompanying Christ, staying with him, demands coming out of ourselves and being outgoing: to come out of ourselves, out of a dreary way of living faith that has become a habit, out of the temptation to withdraw into our own plans, which end by shutting out God's creative action.

God came out of himself to come among us. He pitched his tent among us to bring us his mercy that saves and gives hope. We must not be satisfied with staying in the pen of the ninety-nine sheep if we want to follow him and remain with him. We too must "go out" with him to seek the lost sheep, the one that has strayed the farthest. Always remember that we need to come out of ourselves... just as God came out of himself in Jesus, and Jesus came out of himself for all of us.

Someone might say to me: "But Father, I don't have time." "I have so many things to do." "It's difficult." "What can I do with my weakness and my sins, with so many things?" We are often satisfied with a few prayers, with a distracted and sporadic participation in Sunday Mass, with a few charitable acts, but we do not have the courage "to come out" to bring Christ to others. We are a bit like Saint Peter. As soon as Jesus speaks of his passion, death, and resurrection, of the gift of himself, of love for all, the apostle takes him aside and reproaches him. What Jesus says upsets his plans, seems unacceptable, and threatens the security Peter had built for himself, his idea of the Messiah. And Jesus looks at his disciples and addresses to Peter what may possibly be the harshest words in the Gospels: "Get behind me, Satan! For you are not on the side of God, but of men" (Mark 8:33).

9

# Glory and the Cross

## The Transfiguration (9:1–10)[1]

The gospel passage recounts the event of the transfiguration, which takes place at the height of Jesus's public ministry. He is on his way to Jerusalem, where the prophecies of the "Servant of God" and his redemptive sacrifice are to be fulfilled. The crowds did not understand this. Presented with a messiah who contrasted with their earthly expectations, they abandoned him. They thought the Messiah would be the liberator from Roman domination, the emancipator of the homeland. They do not like Jesus's perspective and so they leave him. Neither do the apostles understand the words with which Jesus proclaims the outcome of his mission in the glorious passion. They do not understand!

Jesus thus chooses to give to Peter, James, and John a foretaste of his glory, which he will have after the resurrection, in order to confirm them in faith and encourage them to follow him on the trying path, on the way of the cross. On a high mountain, immersed in prayer, he is transfigured before them; his face and his entire person radiate a blinding light. The three disciples are frightened as a cloud envelops them and the Father's voice sounds from above, as at the baptism at the Jordan: "This is my beloved Son; listen to him" (Mark 9:7). Jesus is the Son-made-Servant, sent into the world to save us all through the cross, fulfilling the plan of salvation. His full adherence to God's will renders his humanity transparent to the glory of God, who is love.

Jesus thus reveals himself as the perfect icon of the Father, the radiance of his glory. He is the fulfillment of revelation. That is why Moses and Elijah appear beside him. They represent the law and the prophets, so as to signify that everything finishes and begins in Jesus, in his passion and in his glory.

The Father's instruction for the disciples and for us is this: "Listen to him!" Listen to Jesus. He is the Savior. Follow him! To listen to Christ, in fact, entails taking up the logic of his paschal mystery, setting out on the journey with him to make of oneself a gift of love to others in obedience to the will of God, with an attitude of detachment from worldly things, an attitude of interior freedom. One must, in other words, be willing to "lose one's very life" (cf. Mark 8:35) by giving it up so that all might be saved. Thus, we will meet in eternal happiness. The path to Jesus always leads us to happiness. Don't forget this! Jesus's way always leads us to happiness. There will always be a cross and trials throughout, but in the end we are always led to happiness. Jesus does not deceive us. He promised us happiness and will give it to us if we follow his ways.

Along with Peter, James, and John, we too climb the Mount of the transfiguration today and stop in contemplation of the face of Jesus to retrieve the message and translate it into our lives, for we too can be transfigured by Love.

## Jesus Leads Us Home (9:14–29)[2]

Jesus was coming down the mountain where he had been transfigured and found himself among a restless, disorderly crowd that was arguing and shouting. When Jesus asked them what had happened, the restless din quieted, and he began to speak with the father of a boy who was possessed while all of the onlookers listened in silence. When at last Jesus freed him, the boy was like a corpse—so much so that many people believed him dead. But Jesus took him by the hand, lifted him up, and had him stand. The boy was finally healed and could return home with his family.

All the disorder and the discussion ended in a gesture: Jesus bent down and took the child by the hand. The gestures of Jesus make us reflect. In fact, when Jesus heals, when he goes among the people and heals a person, he never leaves the person alone.... He is not a magician, warlock, or a healer who goes and heals and then continues on his way. Rather, he first has everyone return to their proper place and does not leave anyone on the road alone.

There are several beautiful gestures of the Lord that we find narrated in the Gospel. Consider the small girl, Jairus's daughter. When Jesus brings her back to life, he looks at her parents and says: "Give her something to eat!" He reassures the girl's father, as if saying to him: "Your daughter is returning home, she is returning to her family." He acted in the same way with Lazarus, when he came out of the tomb, and with the dead boy, whose widowed mother followed behind the coffin: the Lord raised the boy and gave him back to his mother.

Jesus always has us return home; he never leaves us on the road alone. We also find this in the parables. For example, the lost coin ended up in the widow's purse with the others, and the lost sheep was brought back to the herd with the others.

Jesus is the son of a people. He is the promise made to a people. Jesus's gestures teach us that every healing, every act of forgiveness, always brings us back to our people, that is, to the Church.

Many times, Jesus used inexplicable gestures . . . with those who had been distanced from the community after having been condemned by their fellow citizens. Among them, we find Zacchaeus, who really was a crook and a traitor to his country. And yet Jesus rejoices over him. And we think of Matthew, another traitor to the homeland, who gave money to the Romans. Here again, Jesus goes to a feast at his home: a wonderful meal! We learn that when Jesus forgives he always has us return home. Therefore, we cannot understand Jesus without understanding the people of his origin, God's chosen people, the people of Israel. And we cannot understand him without understanding the people he has called to himself, that is, the Church.

We recall a saying of Paul VI: "It is absurd to love Christ without the Church, to listen to Christ but not to the Church, to follow Christ on the margins of the Church." Christ and the Church are one. The deepest and greatest theology speaks to us of a wedding: Christ the Bridegroom, the Church the Bride. Each time Christ calls a person, he leads that person to the Church. Just think of a child who comes to be baptized. He receives baptism in Mother Church, who accompanies her children and leaves them in the hands of the other Mother of the last moments of life, our Mother and the Mother of Jesus.

Jesus's tender gestures enable us to understand that our doctrine—our following of Christ—is not an idea. It is a continual abiding at home. And if it is a possibility, and a reality, for each of us to leave home through a sin or a mistake . . . salvation comes in returning home: with Jesus in the Church. Therefore, through these one-to-one gestures of tenderness, the Lord calls us into his people, into his family: our Mother, the holy Church.

Let us imagine how Jesus acted with so many people whom he encountered along the way. They were "little gestures" but they were "gestures of tenderness which speak to us of a people, of a family, of a mother. And they remind us that the salvation that Jesus brings always leads us home. We ask our Mother, Our Lady, for the grace to understand this mystery.

## Two Languages, Two Lifestyles (9:30–37)[3]

Scripture presents Jesus who was teaching his disciples and telling them the truth about a proper life—about his own life, but also about the life of Christians, the "true" path. He revealed that the Son of Man would be delivered into the hands of men; they would kill him; and after three days he would rise.

Confronted with this truth—"I have come for this task, to fulfill this mission: to give my life for the salvation of all"—the disciples did not understand. Indeed, they did not want to understand, and as they were afraid to ask, they decided to let it go, as if to say: "Things will take care of themselves." Fear closed their hearts to the truth that Jesus was teaching them.

### *Two languages*

When they arrived in Capernaum, Jesus asked: "What were you discussing on the way?" There was no answer. Indeed, they were ashamed to tell Jesus what they were discussing. Along the way, in fact, they were discussing who among them was the greatest.

Here, then, is the juxtaposition: Jesus speaks a language of humiliation, of death, of redemption, and they speak a language of climbers: Who will climb the highest in terms of power? This is a temptation that they had—they were tempted by a worldly way of thinking—but they were not the only ones. The mother of James and John, too, went to Jesus (cf. Matt 20:20–21) to ask that one of her sons be seated on his right and the other on his left when he arrived in the kingdom. As if she were to ask today that one be prime minister and the other the minister of the economy, so as to share all the power. For this very reason, the question: "Who is the greatest?" is worldly thinking. Therefore Jesus takes care to tell them: "If anyone would be first, he must be last of all and servant of all."

Jesus's words to the disciples are a lesson for everyone. On the path that Jesus points out to us in order to go forward, service is the rule. The one who is greatest is the one who serves, who is most at the service of others, not the one who boasts, who seeks power, money, vanity, and pride. This lesson is important, because it is a story that happens every day in the Church, in every community where it is often asked: "Who is the greatest among us? Who is in charge?" This is how ambitions emerge, along with the desire to climb, to have power....

Jesus, on the one hand, speaks a language of service, of humility. He says: "I have not come... to be served, but to serve." On the other hand, the language of the world asks: "Who has more power to command?" This worldly language is in opposition to God, as, for example, when there is vanity and the worldly desire to have power, not to serve, but to be served. We all know how gossip, speaking badly about others, is motivated by envy and jealousy that lead us down this path of destruction.

All this happens today in every institution of the Church: parishes, colleges, and other institutions, even in dioceses ... everywhere. These are the two ways of speaking: on the one hand, there is the worldly spirit, which is the spirit of wealth, vanity, and pride. On the other hand, Jesus said: "The Son of man will be delivered into the hands of men, and they will kill him." He came to serve and he taught us that the way of Christian life is service and humility. After all, when the great saints said they felt they were sinners, it was because they understood this worldly spirit that was inside them, and they had many worldly temptations. Indeed, none of us can say: "No, not me, not me...I am a holy, clean person." We are all tempted by these things. We are tempted to destroy others in order to climb higher. It is a worldly temptation that divides and destroys the Church, and it is certainly not the Spirit of Jesus.

## Worldly Temptations (9:30–37)[4]

The Book of Sirach (2:1–13) states: "My son, when you come to serve the Lord, prepare yourself for testing. Set your heart right and be steadfast" (cf. vv. 1–2). Christian life is a life with temptation and, therefore, we must be prepared for temptation because we will all be tempted.

This is confirmed in the Gospel of Mark (9:30–37), which indicates that Jesus went with his disciples decisively, resolutely, toward Jerusalem in order to fulfill his mission of doing the Father's will. Jesus informed the disciples in advance of what would happen in Jerusalem: "The Son of man will be delivered into the hands of men, and they will kill him; and when he is killed, after three days he will rise." Not even the disciples understood these words, and they were afraid to ask him to explain, so they said: "Let's stop here. It's better." In other words, they gave in to the temptation not to fulfill the mission, a temptation to which Jesus was also subjected at least twice. The first time was in the desert, with the devil's three propositions. ...Another time, it was Peter who tempted him when, as Jesus spoke of his fate, Peter said: "No, this will never happen, Lord!" To him too, Jesus replied, "Begone, Satan!" Indeed, Peter was doing the same thing that the devil, Satan, had done in the desert.

Interestingly, the disciples did not want to hear these words of Jesus. They did not understand these words and were afraid to ask him. The disciples' difficulty is further clarified later in the reading. "When they arrived in Capernaum, Jesus asked them: 'What were you discussing on the way?'" Here, too, they were silent." But this time they were silent out of shame. Indeed, whereas the first time they were "afraid" and repeated, "No, let's not ask anything more: it's better to keep quiet," this time, they felt ashamed because along the way they had discussed with one another who was the greatest. They were ashamed of this discussion. It was a twofold attitude: that of fear and that of shame. They were good people who wanted to follow the Lord, to serve the Lord. But they did not know that the way of serving the Lord was not very easy. It was not like enlisting in something, like a charitable association. For this reason, they were afraid; they fell into the temptation of worldliness.

***The Church today***

The temptation was not theirs alone. From the moment that the Church became the Church up until today, this has happened. It happens and will continue to happen. For example, it happens in parishes where there are always struggles, and one might hear someone say: "I want to be president of this association, I will try to climb a little"; or "Who is the greatest one here? Who is the greatest one in this parish? No, I am more important than he is, and that man there is not because he did something...." The temptation to worldliness is where the chain of sins begins, sins such as speaking ill of others and gossiping, which are all things that serve one who seeks to "climb."

It is a temptation from which the clergy are not exempt. At times, we priests say, shamefully: "I would like that parish..." or "The Lord is here, but I would prefer to be there...." In other words, we follow not the path of the Lord, but that of vanity, of worldliness. Even among us bishops, the same thing happens: worldliness comes as a temptation. And so it happens that a bishop can say: "I am in this diocese but I would like that one, which is more important," and he tries to make an impression, to influence, to push in order to get there. In short, the mission is to serve the Lord, but often our real desire pushes us toward the path of worldliness in order to be more important. Then there may be disappointment, as was the case for Jesus's disciples, who first kept quiet out of fear and then remained silent out of shame. Let us ask the Lord for the grace to be ashamed when we find ourselves in these situations.

### *The choice*

The criterion for choosing our actions in the face of certain temptations is explained by Jesus in the same gospel passage: "He sat down and said to them, 'If anyone would be first, he must be last of all and servant of all,'" and, taking a child in his arms, he said: "Become as this child." Christ overturned everything—glory and the cross, greatness and the child.

This is a gospel passage that leads us to pray for the Church, to pray for all of us that the Lord may protect us from ambition, from the worldliness of feeling that we are greater than others. Lord, grant us the grace of shame, of holy shame, when we find ourselves in that situation. Grant us the grace to say: "Am I capable of thinking this way? When I see my Lord on the cross, do I want to use the Lord in order to climb?" Lord, give us the grace of childlike simplicity, of understanding the importance of the path of service and, at the end of a life of service, be able to say: "I am an unworthy servant."

## Who Is the Most Important? (9:30–37)[5]

Who is the most important? This is a lifelong question to which, at different times, we must give an answer. We cannot escape the question; it is written on our hearts. I remember more than once, at family gatherings, children being asked: "Who do you love more, Mommy or Daddy?" It's like asking them: "Who is the most important for you?" But is this only a game we play with children? The history of humanity has been marked by the answer we give to this question.

Jesus is not afraid of people's questions; he is not afraid of our humanity or the different things we are looking for. On the contrary, he knows the depths of the human heart and, as a good teacher, he is always ready to encourage and support us. As usual, he takes up our searching, our aspirations, and he gives them a new horizon. He somehow finds the answers that can pose new challenges, setting aside the "right answers," the standard replies we are expected to give. As usual, Jesus sets before us the logic of love—a mindset, an approach to life, that is capable of being lived by all, because it is meant for all.

Far from any kind of elitism, the horizon to which Jesus points is not for those few privileged souls capable of attaining the heights of knowledge or elevated levels of spirituality. The horizon to which Jesus points always has to do with daily life... with that which can season our daily lives with eternity.

Who is the most important? Jesus is straightforward: "Whoever wishes to be the first—the most important—among you must be the last of all, and the servant of all." Whoever wishes to be great must serve others, not be served by others.

This is the great paradox of Jesus. The disciples were arguing about who would have the highest place, who would be chosen for special privileges. They were the disciples, those closest to Jesus, and they were arguing about that! Who would be above the common law, the general norm, to stand out in the quest for superiority over others? Who would climb the ladder most quickly to take the jobs that carry the greatest benefits?

Jesus upsets their logic, their mindset, simply by telling them that life is lived authentically in a concrete commitment to our neighbor, in other words, by serving.

### *Serving others*

The call to serve involves something special, to which we must be attentive. Serving means caring for another's vulnerability: caring for the vulnerable of our families, our society, our people. Theirs are the suffering, fragile, and downcast faces which Jesus tells us specifically to look at and which he asks us to love with a love that takes shape in our actions and decisions, and that finds expression in whatever tasks we, as citizens, are called to perform. It is people of flesh and blood, people with individual lives and stories and with all their frailty, that Jesus asks us to protect, to care for, and to serve. Being a Christian entails promoting the dignity of our brothers and sisters, fighting for it, and living for it. That is why Christians are constantly called to set aside their own wishes and desires—their pursuit of power—before the actual gaze of those who are most vulnerable.

There is a kind of "service" that serves others, yet we need to be careful not to be tempted by another kind of service, one that is "self-serving" with regard to others. There is a way to go about serving that is interested in helping only *"my people," "our people."* This service always leaves *"your people"* outside, and gives rise to a process of exclusion.

All of us are called by virtue of our Christian vocation to that service which truly serves, and to help one another not to be tempted by a "service" which is really "self-serving." All of us are asked, indeed urged, by Jesus to care for one another out of love without looking to one side or the other to see what our neighbor is doing or not doing. Jesus says: "Whoever would be first among you must be the last, and the servant of all. That person will be the first." Jesus does not say: If your neighbor wants to be first, let him be the servant! We have to be careful to avoid judgmental looks and renew our belief in the transformation to which Jesus invites us.

Caring for others out of love is not about being servile. Rather, it means putting our brothers and sisters at the center.

Service always sees their faces, touches their flesh, senses their closeness, and even, in some cases, "suffers" that closeness and tries to help them. Service is never ideological, for we do not serve ideas, we serve people.

Today, I invite you to care for your vocation, to care for these gifts which God has given you, but, above all, I invite you to care for and be at the service of the frailty of your brothers and sisters. Do not neglect them for plans that can be seductive but have nothing to do with the need of the person beside you. We know, we are witnesses of the incomparable power of the resurrection, which "everywhere calls forth the seeds of a new world" (cf. *Evangelii Gaudium*, 276, 278).

Let us not forget the Good News we have heard today: the importance of a people, a nation, and the importance of individuals, which is always based on how they seek to serve their vulnerable brothers and sisters. Here we encounter one of the fruits of a true humanity.

Because, dear brothers and sisters: "whoever does not live to serve, does not serve to live."

## Our Response (9:33)[7]

The Lord's question—"What were you arguing about along the way?" (Mark 9:33)—might also apply to us. When Jesus put this question to his disciples they were silent; they were ashamed, for they had been arguing about who was the greatest among them. We too feel ashamed when we ponder the distance between the Lord's call and our meager response. Beneath his merciful gaze, we cannot claim that our division is anything less than a scandal and an obstacle to our proclaiming the Gospel of salvation to the world. Our vision is often blurred by the cumulative burden of our divisions, and our will is not always free of that human ambition which can accompany even our desire to preach the Gospel as the Lord commanded (cf. Matt 28:19).

## Welcoming Others (9:37)[7]

"Whoever welcomes one such child in my name welcomes me, and whoever welcomes me welcomes not me but the one who sent me" (Mark 9:37; cf. Matt 18:5; Luke 9:48; John 13:20). With these words, the evangelists remind the Christian community of Jesus's teaching, which both inspires and challenges. This phrase traces the sure path that leads to God; it begins with the smallest and, through the grace of our Savior, it grows into the practice of welcoming others. To be welcoming is a necessary condition for making this journey a concrete reality. God made himself one of us. In Jesus, God became a child, and the openness of faith to God, which nourishes hope, is expressed in loving proximity to the smallest and the weakest. Charity, faith, and hope are all actively present in the spiritual and corporal works of mercy....

But the evangelists reflect also on the responsibility of the one who works against mercy: "If any of you put a stumbling block before one of these little ones who believe in me, it would be better for you if a great millstone were hung around your neck and you were thrown into the sea" (Mark 9:42; cf. Matt 18:6; Luke 17:2). How can we ignore this severe warning when we see the exploitation carried out by unscrupulous people? Such exploitation harms young girls and boys who are led into prostitution or into the mire of pornography; who are enslaved as child laborers or soldiers; who are caught up in drug trafficking and other forms of criminality; and who are forced to flee from conflict and persecution, risking isolation and abandonment.

## The Secret to a Good Life (9:37)[8]

In places such as this, we are all confirmed in the faith; each one is helped in his or her belief because we see the faith visibly expressed in practical acts of charity. We see how faith brings light and hope in situations of grave hardship. We observe how faith is rekindled in hearts touched by the Spirit of Jesus, who said, "Whoever welcomes one such child in my name welcomes me" (Mark 9:37). This faith, working through charity, dislodges mountains of indifference, disbelief, and apathy, and opens hands and hearts to work for what is good and share this experience. Through humble gestures and simple acts of service to the least among us, the Good News that Jesus is risen and lives among us is proclaimed.

Goodness is its own reward and draws us closer to God, who is the Supreme Good. It helps us to think like him, to see our lives in the light of his plan of love for each one of us. Goodness enables us to delight in life's daily joys, helping us in difficulties and trials. Goodness offers infinitely more than money, which only deludes, because we have been created to receive the love of God and to offer it, not measuring everything in terms of money or power, which is the danger that kills us all. . . .

The secret to a good life is found in loving and in giving oneself for love's sake. From here comes the strength to "sacrifice oneself joyfully," and thus the most demanding work is transformed into a source of a greater joy. In this way, there is no longer any fear of making important choices in life, but they are seen for what they are, namely, as the way to personal fulfillment in freedom.

## Do Not Delay Conversion (9:41–50)[9]

The word "sin" comes up four times in this passage, and the Lord is very harsh in using it. Jesus says, "If any of you put a stumbling block before one of these little ones who believe in me, it would be better for you if a great millstone were hung around your neck and you were thrown into the sea." In fact, for the Lord, sin is the same as destruction. This is why Jesus advises that it is better to destroy yourself than to destroy others. "Cut off your hand, cut off your foot, pluck out your eye, throw yourself into the sea," but do not cause the little ones, that is, the just ones, those who trust in the Lord, who simply believe in the Lord, to sin.

### *The double life*

What is sin? The answer to this question affects every person's actual life. Sin is saying one thing and doing another; it is a double life. For example, I am very Catholic, I always go to Mass, I belong to this association and another; but my life is not Christian: I do not pay my employees fairly; I take advantage of people; I play dirty in business; I launder money. This is a double life, and unfortunately there are many Catholics who are like this and cause sin.

The words of Jesus are clear, and they bring each of us to reflect on our daily lives. How many times have we heard, in our neighborhood or elsewhere, that "it is better to be an atheist than to be a Catholic like him." This is sin, which destroys, and which wears us down. It happens every day: just watch the television news or read the newspapers. There are many scandals in newspapers. Scandals spread, and they destroy.

There was an important company that was on the verge of bankruptcy. Since the authorities wanted to avoid a strike, which was justified but which would also have resolved nothing, they tried to get in touch with the company's director. But where was this person while the company was failing and people were not receiving wages for their work? This manager, who claimed to be a very Catholic man, was on a beach in the Middle East having a winter holiday. This fact never made it to the papers, but people found out. These are the sins—the double lives—that Jesus is referring to when he asks those who behave like this not to destroy, with their double lives, the little ones who believe in him.

***Examination of conscience***

Imagine the moment when the sinner knocks on heaven's door: "It is I, Lord!"—Don't you remember? I used to go to church, I was close to you. I belonged to this and that association. I did this . . . do you not recall all my offerings?

"Yes, I remember. The offerings I recall. All of them were dirty. You stole them all from the poor. I do not know you." . . .

It would be good for each one of us to think about whether there is a double life within us—to appear just, to appear as good believers, good Catholics, but to really be doing something else. It is a case of trying to find out if our behavior is that of someone who says, "The Lord will forgive me everything, so I will continue . . ."; someone who, despite being aware of their mistakes, says: "Yes, this is no good. I will convert, but not today. No. Tomorrow." An examination of conscience that leads to a conversion of heart begins by acknowledging that "sin destroys."

## The Scandal of Inconsistency (9:41–50)[10]

We need to think like Christians, to feel like Christians, and to act like Christians. Consistency in the Christian life means that in one's acting, feeling, and thinking one acknowledges the presence of the Lord.

When one of these [characteristics] is missing ... one is not a Christian. One might say, "I am a Christian!" But if you do not live like a Christian, if you do not act like a Christian, if you do not think like a Christian and feel like a Christian, something is amiss. There is a certain inconsistency! All Christians are called to give testimony to Jesus Christ. And Christians who ordinarily and generally live inconsistently do great harm....

The life of a Christian is found in consistency; and yet we also need to be aware of the temptation not to be consistent, and to cause great scandal. And scandal destroys!

The consequences are there for all to see. Everyone has heard it said: "I believe in God but not in the Church, because you Christians say one thing and do another!" These are words that we have all heard: "I believe in God but not in you!" And this occurs precisely because of inconsistency.

To act, feel, and think as Christians we need to pray that we may live a consistent Christian life, for Christian consistency is a gift of God. It is a gift we should ask for, saying: "Lord, may I be consistent! Lord, may I never give scandal!" Let us be people who think like Christians, feel like Christians, and act like Christians!"

If you happen to be with an atheist who tells you that he does not believe in God, you can read him the whole library where it says that God exists, and where it is proven that God exists, and yet he will not believe. However, if in the presence of this same atheist you live a consistent, Christian life, something will begin to work in his heart. And it will be your witness that brings him the restlessness on which the Holy Spirit works.

All of us, the whole Church, should ask the Lord for the grace to be consistent. This means acknowledging ourselves as sinners, weak and inconsistent, but always ready to ask for the Lord's forgiveness. All of us, in fact, are able to ask for forgiveness, and God never tires of forgiving. It is important, then, to have the humility to ask for forgiveness when we have not been consistent.

In the end, it is a matter of proceeding forward in life with Christian consistency by testifying that we believe in Jesus Christ and by acknowledging that we are sinners. We must have the courage to ask for forgiveness when we have made mistakes and fear that we have given scandal. Let us pray that the Lord may give all of us this grace.

10

# Discipleship

## Marriage (10:1–12)[1]

Jesus, who reconciled all things in himself, restored marriage and the family to their original form (cf. Mark 10:1–12). Marriage and the family have been redeemed by Christ (cf. Eph 5:21–32) and restored in the image of the Holy Trinity, the mystery from which all true love flows. The spousal covenant, originating in creation and revealed in the history of salvation, takes on its full meaning in Christ and his Church. Through his Church, Christ bestows on marriage and the family the grace necessary to bear witness to the love of God and to live the life of communion.

"The Gospel of the family spans the history of the world, from the creation of man and woman in the image and likeness of God (cf. Gen 1:26–27) to the fulfillment of the mystery of the covenant in Christ at the end of time with the marriage of the Lamb (cf. Rev 19:9)."[2]

## Justice and Mercy (10:1–12)[3]

There were three groups of people who followed Jesus (Mark 10:1–12). Thus, *the crowd* followed him in order to learn, for he spoke with authority. Of course, they also followed him in order to be healed. The second group comprised *the doctors of the law,* who instead followed him in order to put him to the test. They approached and asked questions in order to test him. Then there were *the disciples,* the third group. They followed him because they were drawn to him. Jesus himself had called them to be near him. And thus, these three groups were always following Jesus.

Mark informs us that Jesus was approached by the doctors of the law. The Gospel clearly states that, in order to test him, they asked Jesus if it was lawful for a husband to disavow his wife. But Jesus did not answer whether it was lawful or not; he did not enter into their casuistic logic, because they thought of the faith only in terms of "you can" or "you cannot"—to what point "you can" and to what point "you cannot." Jesus instead asked them a question: "What did Moses command you?" In other words, "What is in your law?"

In answering the question posed by Jesus, the doctors of the law explain the permission Moses gave for divorcing one's wife, and it is they who fall into the snare, because Jesus describes them as "hard of heart." Thus, Jesus speaks the truth, without casuistry, without permissions, simply the truth: "From the beginning of creation, God made them male and female." And he continues: "For this reason, a man shall leave his father and mother" and set out on a journey, and be "joined to his wife, and the two shall become one flesh." Therefore, "they are no longer two, but one flesh." And this is neither casuistry nor permission: it is the truth. Jesus always speaks the truth.

***The disciples***

Mark then describes the reaction of the third group—the disciples—at home. They questioned him again on this subject so as to better understand, because they knew about this permission of Moses, this law of Moses. And Jesus was even clearer: "Whoever divorces his wife and marries another commits adultery against her" (v. 11).

Thus, Jesus speaks the truth. He avoids casuistic logic and explains things as they were created; he explains the truth. But surely, one may think: "Yes, this is the truth, but you, Jesus, spoke with an adulteress!" Furthermore, she was an adulteress many times over: five, I believe. In doing so, you became unclean. And you also became unclean because that woman was a pagan; she was a Samaritan. And speaking with one who was not a Jew made you unclean. Moreover, you drank from the glass of one who had not been purified. Thus, why do you say that this is adultery, that this is grave, and then you speak with that woman, you explain the catechism to her and also drink what she gives you? Indeed, they once brought you an adulteress—clear to everyone: they caught her in adultery—and, in the end, what did you say? "I do not condemn you, do not sin again." One might ask, "How do you explain this?"

It is the Christian journey. It is the journey of Jesus, because he ate with sinners. Let us not forget the tax collector Matthew, and Zacchaeus, and all the sinners with whom Jesus ate. Jesus's journey is clear; it is the journey from casuistry to the truth and to mercy: Jesus avoids casuistry, and those who wish to put him to the test—those who think with this "you can" logic—he defines—not here, but in another gospel passage—as hypocrites. This also applies to the fourth commandment: these men refused to take care of their parents, with the excuse that they had given a nice offering to the Church—hypocrites! Casuistry is hypocritical thinking: "you can; you cannot." A thought that can then become more subtle, more evil: "Up to this point, I can, but beyond this, I cannot," which is the deception of casuistry. Instead, we must turn from casuistry to truth. And, this is the truth. Jesus does not negotiate truth, ever: he always and only speaks the truth.

But there is not only truth, there is also mercy, because he is the incarnation of the Father's mercy and cannot deny himself.... And this is the path that Jesus teaches us to take. Life is not easy when temptations arrive. Let us consider temptations in business where we say: "I can do so up to here; I'll fire these employees and earn more over there." This is "casuistry." Indeed, when temptations reach the heart, this journey to escape from casuistry to truth and to mercy is not easy. It takes the grace of God, which helps us to go forth in this way. And we must always ask for this grace.

## God Is Not an Equation (10:1–12)[4]

Jesus, having departed from Capernaum, "went to the region of Judea and beyond the Jordan," and "crowds again gathered around him; and, as was his custom, he again taught them" (v. 1).

The protagonist is the crowd that comes to him: he taught them and they listened. All of those people followed Jesus precisely because they enjoyed listening to him. The Gospel says that "he taught with authority, not as the scribes and Pharisees taught." This is why the crowd, the people of God, was with Jesus.

However there was also, on the other side, that small group of Pharisees, Sadducees, and doctors of the law who were always approaching Jesus with bad intentions. The Gospel clearly tells us that their intention was to test him; they were always ready to use the classic banana peel to trip Jesus up, thus taking away his "authority."

These people were separated from the people of God. They were a small group of enlightened theologians who believed that they had all knowledge and wisdom. But, in elaborating their theology, they fell into casuistry, and could not get out of the trap of constantly repeating: "You cannot, you cannot!" . . .

Twice in the Gospel this small group addresses Jesus on the subject of marriage. The Sadducees, who did not believe in eternal life, posed a question about levirate marriage, that is, the woman who was married to seven brothers and then eventually died: which one will be her husband in the afterlife? It was a question that was formulated precisely in order to ridicule Jesus.

Their other question was: "Is it lawful to divorce a woman?" However, in both situations, Jesus does not stop at the particular case. Instead, he goes further. He focuses on the fullness of marriage.

In the case of levirate, Jesus speaks of eschatological fullness: "In heaven there will be neither husband nor wife, they will live like angels of God." He moves to the fullness of light that comes from eschatological fullness. Therefore, Jesus reminds us of the fullness of creation: "From the beginning of creation, God made them male and female."

It is clear that he is not wrong. He is not trying to make a good impression. He simply says, "God made them male and female." Immediately, he adds: "For this reason a man shall leave his father and mother and be joined to his wife, and the woman shall leave her father and mother and be joined to her husband—it is understood—and the two shall become one flesh." This is powerful: a symbiosis, one flesh; they are no longer two, but one flesh. Therefore, "what God has joined together let not man put asunder."

In both this case and that of levirate, Jesus responds with the overwhelming truth, the blunt truth—this is the truth!—of fullness, always. After all, Jesus never negotiates the truth. This small group of enlightened theologians always negotiates truth, reducing it to a case study. Jesus, on the contrary, does not negotiate truth: this is the truth about marriage, and there is no other.

### *Mercy*

However, Jesus is so merciful, and so great that never, never, never does he close the door to sinners. You can see this when he asks them: "What did Moses command you? What did Moses command you?" The answer is that "Moses permitted the writing of an act of repudiation." And it's true; it's true. But Jesus responds: "It was because of your hardness of heart that he wrote this rule for you."

Here we have the fullness of truth, the truth that is powerful and blunt, but there is also human weakness and hardness of heart. And Moses, the legislator, did this, but things remain clear: the truth is one thing, while hardness of heart is another, the sinful condition of us all. Therefore, Jesus leaves the door open here to God's forgiveness, but to the disciples, he repeats the truth: "Whoever divorces his wife and marries another commits adultery." Jesus is clear and forthright: "And if she divorces her husband and marries another, she commits adultery."

The gospel passage speaks to us of the truths that Jesus gives us, which are full truths, given by God, the Father.... It also shows us the way in which Jesus acts before sinners: with forgiveness, leaving the door open. And in this reference to Moses, he leaves a little something for the forgiveness of people who have failed....

Recalling Moses, Jesus tells us that there is hardness of heart, there is sin. But you can do something: forgiveness, understanding, accompaniment, integration, the discernment—with the understanding that truth can never be sold, never. Jesus is able to speak this truth, which is so great, and at the same time he is forgiving toward sinners, toward the weak.

However, this small group of enlightened theologians, who are locked into their legalistic approach, are both incapable of great horizons and of loving and understanding human weakness.

We must walk with these two things that Jesus teaches us: truth and understanding. And this cannot be resolved like a mathematical equation, but with flesh itself. In other words, as a Christian I help that person, I help those marriages that are facing difficulty, that are wounded, on their path to approaching God. The fact remains that that is the truth, but this is another truth: we are all sinners, on the road. And there is always this work to do: helping, accompanying, but also teaching those who want to get married the truth about marriage.

Curiously, when speaking of the truth, Jesus is clear and forthright, but he treats the adulterers so gently. He acts with gentleness toward the woman whom they brought before him to be stoned. He acts with such gentleness, saying: "Woman, no one has condemned you, and neither do I. Go in peace and sin no more!" With great gentleness Jesus spoke to the Samaritan woman, who had a history of adultery, saying to her: "Go call your husband," to which she responded: "I have no husband."

In conclusion, let us pray that Jesus may teach us to have in our hearts great adherence to truth and also great understanding and support for all of our brothers and sisters who are in difficulty. This is a gift. It is what is taught by the Holy Spirit, not by those enlightened doctors who, in order to teach us, need to reduce the fullness of God to a case study and an equation.

## THE TRINITY (10:10–11)[5]

"Jesus, who reconciled all things in himself and redeemed us from sin, not only returned marriage and the family to their original form, but also raised marriage to the sacramental sign of his love for the Church (cf. Matt 19:1–12; Mark 10:1–12; Eph 5:21–32). In the human family, gathered by Christ, "the image and likeness" of the Most Holy Trinity (cf. Gen 1:26) has been restored, the mystery from which all true love flows. Through the Church, marriage and the family receive the grace of the Holy Spirit from Christ, in order to bear witness to the Gospel of God's love."[6]

## Become Like Children (10:14)[7]

Children remind us that we all, in the first years of life, were completely dependent on the care and benevolence of others. The Son of God was not spared this stage. It is the mystery that we contemplate every year at Christmas. The nativity scene is the icon that communicates this reality in the simplest and most direct way. Interestingly, God has no difficulty in making himself understood by children, and children have no difficulty in understanding God. It is not by chance that in the Gospel there are several very beautiful and powerful words of Jesus regarding the "little ones." This term refers to all the people who depend on the help of others, and to children, in particular. For example, Jesus says: "I thank you, Father, Lord of heaven and earth, because you have hidden these things from the wise and the intelligent and have revealed them to infants" (Matt 11:25). And again: "Take care that you do not despise one of these little ones; for, I tell you, in heaven their angels continually see the face of my Father in heaven" (Matt 18:10).

Thus, children are in and of themselves a treasure for humanity and also for the Church, for they constantly evoke that necessary condition for entering the kingdom of God: that of not considering ourselves self-sufficient, but in need of help, of love, of forgiveness. We all are in need of help, of love, and of forgiveness!

Children remind us of another beautiful thing: they remind us that we are always sons and daughters. Even if one becomes an adult, or an elderly person, even if one becomes a parent, if one occupies a position of responsibility, underneath all of this is still the identity of a child. We are all sons and daughters. And this always brings us to the fact that we did not give ourselves life but that we received it. The great gift of life is the first gift that we received. Sometimes we risk forgetting this, as if we were the masters of our existence; instead, we are fundamentally dependent. In reality, it is a source of great joy to feel at every stage of life, in every situation, in every social condition, that we are and we remain sons and daughters. This is the main message that children give us by their very presence. Simply by their presence they remind us that each and every one of us is a son or daughter.

There are so many gifts, so many riches that children bring to humanity. I shall mention only a few.

They bring their way of seeing reality, with a trusting and pure gaze. A child has spontaneous trust in his father and mother; a spontaneous trust in God, in Jesus, in Our Lady. At the same time, a child's interior gaze is pure, not yet tainted by malice, by duplicity, by the "harshness" of life that hardens the heart. We know that children are also marked by original sin, that they are selfish, and yet they preserve purity and interior simplicity. But children are not diplomats; they say what they feel, say what they see, directly. And so often they cause difficulties for their parents, saying in front of other people: "I don't like this because it is ugly." But children say what they see. They are not two-faced. They have not yet learned the science of duplicity that we adults have unfortunately learned.

Furthermore, children—in their interior simplicity—bring with them the capacity to receive and give tenderness. Tenderness is having a heart "of flesh" and not "of stone," as the Bible says (cf. Ezek 36:26). Tenderness is also poetry: it is "feeling" things and events, not treating them as mere objects, only to use them because they are useful. . . .

Children have the capacity to smile and to cry. Some, when I pick them up to embrace them, smile; others see me dressed in white and think I am a doctor and that I am going to vaccinate them and they cry. . . spontaneously! Children are like this: they smile and cry, two things that are often "stifled" in grown-ups. . . . So often our smile becomes a cardboard smile, fixed, a smile that is not natural, even an artificial smile, like that of a clown. Children smile and cry spontaneously. It always depends on the heart, and often our heart is blocked and loses this capacity to smile, to cry. So children can teach us how to smile and cry again. But we must ask ourselves: Do I smile spontaneously, frankly, with love, or is my smile artificial? Do I still cry or have I lost the capacity to cry? These are two very human questions that children lead us to ask.

For all these reasons Jesus invited his disciples to "become like children," because "the kingdom of God belongs to those who are like them" (cf. Matt 18:3; Mark 10:14).

Dear brothers and sisters, children bring life, cheerfulness, hope, and also troubles. But such is life. Certainly, they can bring worries and sometimes many problems—but better a society with these worries and these problems than a sad, gray society because it is without children! When we see that the birthrate of a society is barely one percent, we can say that this society is sad, it is gray because it has no children.

### The Food of Jesus (10:17–22)[8]

To do the will of God is the food of Jesus, and it is also the Christian path. . . . It isn't easy. Recall the story of the rich young man in the Gospels of Matthew (19:16–22) and Mark (10:17–22). . . . Jesus proposed something to the young man, but he didn't have courage. This is why, when the Father, when Jesus asks something of us, we need to ask ourselves: "Is this God's will?" Of course, we may feel challenged and not really capable, with our strength, of accepting what the Lord asks of us. But we can find help by praying: "Lord, give me the courage to go forth according to the Father's will."

And the Lord gives us all the grace so that one day he may say of us what he said of that group, of that crowd who followed him, those who were seated around him: "Here are my mother and my brethren! Whoever does the will of God is my brother and sister and mother" (Mark 3:34–35). In doing God's will, we become part of Jesus's family. It makes us mother, father, sister, brother. We ask that the Lord will give us the grace of this familiarity with him, a familiarity that means actually doing God's will.

## True Riches (10:17–22)[9]

Once I asked you the question: "Where is your treasure?" Where does your heart find its rest?... Our hearts can be attached to true or false treasures. They can find genuine rest or they can simply slumber, becoming lazy and lethargic. The greatest good we can have in life is our relationship with God. Are you convinced of this? Do you realize how much you are worth in the eyes of God? Do you know that you are loved and welcomed by him unconditionally, just as you are? Once we lose our sense of this, we become an incomprehensible enigma, for it is the knowledge that we are loved unconditionally by God that gives meaning to our lives. Do you remember the conversation that Jesus had with the rich young man (cf. Mark 10:17–22)? The evangelist Mark observes that the Lord looked upon him and loved him (v. 21) and invited him to follow him to find true riches.

## Enchanted by the Serpent (10:17–27)[10]

This passage from Mark (10:17–27) that speaks of the young rich man could be entitled, "The Journey from Joy and Hope to Sorrow and Isolation." Indeed, the young man wants to follow Jesus, sees him and runs to him, thrilled to ask him a question: "What must I do to inherit eternal life?" After an appeal to follow the commandments, the Lord exhorts him: "You lack one thing; go, sell what you own, and give the money to the poor, and you will have treasure in heaven; then come, follow me." When he heard this, the young man's countenance fell, and he "went away grieving, for he had many possessions."

### *Living without a horizon*

From enthusiasm to sorrow: He wanted to go with Jesus but he left by another path. The reason? He was attached to his possessions. He had many possessions. And in the final analysis, the possessions won. Jesus reacted: He said to his disciples with conviction: "How hard it will be for those who have wealth to enter the kingdom of God." Indeed, there is a mystery in the possession of wealth. Riches have the capacity to seduce, to lead us to us believe we are in an earthly paradise. I recall that in the 1970s I saw for the first time a gated community of people who were wealthy. It was closed to protect against thieves, to be secure. There were also good people there, but they were enclosed in that sort of "earthly paradise." This happens when we close ourselves off to protect our possessions. We lose the horizon. And living without a horizon is sad.

Things that are closed become ruined; they become corrupt. Attachment to riches is the start of every kind of corruption, everywhere: personal corruption, corruption in business, even small corruption in commerce—such as that of those who subtract a few ounces from the correct weight of merchandise—political corruption, corruption in education. . . . So many live their lives attached to their own power, to their riches, believing they are in paradise. They are closed, they have no horizon, and they have no hope. In the end they will have to leave it all.

### *Living without hope*

Recall the parable where Jesus speaks to the man who wore elegant clothes and feasted lavishly every day. He was so closed within himself that he no longer could see past the end of his nose: he didn't notice that there, at the gate to his house, was a man who was hungry, sick, and covered in sores. The same thing happens to us. Attachment to riches makes us believe that all is well, that there is an earthly paradise—but it takes away our hope and our horizon. And living with no horizon is a barren life; living without hope is a sad life.

However, this is a criticism of "attachment," not of "good management of riches." In fact, riches are for the common good, for all, and if the Lord grants them to someone, it is for the good of all, not for oneself, not to close up one's heart, which then becomes corrupt and sorrowful. Jesus uses a powerful expression: "How hard it will be for those who have riches to enter the kingdom of God." Riches are like the serpent in the earthly paradise: they beguile, they deceive, and they make us believe we are powerful, like God. In the end, they take away the best, which is hope, and lead us to the worst, into corruption. This is why Jesus states: "It is easier for a camel to go through the eye of a needle than for someone who is rich to enter the kingdom of God."

Here there is valuable advice for everyone: those who possess riches need to refer to the first Beatitude: "Blessed are the poor in spirit." In other words, detach yourself from this attachment and let the riches that the Lord has given be for the common good. The only way to act is to open your hand, open your heart—open the horizon. If your hand is closed, your heart is closed like that of the man who had banquets and dressed in luxurious clothing—you have no horizons. You don't see others who are needy and you will end up like that man: far from God. The same thing happened to the young rich man. He had the path to happiness, he sought it and . . . he lost everything. Because of his attachment to possessions he ended up defeated.

We must ask Jesus for the grace not to be attached to possessions in order not to run the risk of a closed heart, corruption, and barrenness.

## A Person of Wonder (10:17–27)[11]

A young man approached Jesus in order to follow him. He was a "good young man," capable of winning over the heart of Jesus, who, we read, "fixed his gaze upon him" and "loved him." Jesus said to this young man: "There is one thing you lack: sell all that you have, give everything to the poor and come, follow me"; but upon hearing these words the man's "face fell and he went away sorrowful."

The young man was unable to open his heart to joy and chose sadness. Why was this? The answer is clear: because he had many possessions. He was attached to possessions. Furthermore, Jesus himself warned that one cannot serve two masters: you either serve the Lord or you serve riches. Now, riches are not bad in themselves, but it is bad when one serves those riches. And so it was that the young man went away sad: "He went away sorrowful."

This scene also sheds light upon daily life in our parishes, communities, and institutions. Indeed, if we find people who say they are Christian, and want to be Christian, but are sad, it means that something is not right. It is the duty of everyone to help these people find Jesus, to take away that sadness so that they may rejoice in the Gospel and have the joy which is truly of the Gospel.

Before revelation, before the love of God, before the emotions of the Holy Spirit, a Christian is a man or woman of wonder and astonishment.

One word—"astonishment"—also returns at the end of today's gospel passage, when Jesus explains to the apostles how this good young man could not follow him, because he was attached to riches, and says that it is very difficult for the rich, those who are attached to riches, to enter the kingdom of heaven. We read that they were "astonished" and asked: "Who can be saved?"

A person, a Christian, can be so astonished before such greatness and beauty that he or she might think: "I cannot do it. I do not know how to do it!" But looking at his disciples' faces, Jesus consoles them: "It is impossible for men—man cannot do it—but it is not so for God!" We can, therefore, live "Christian joy," be saved from a life attached to things, to worldliness, only with the strength of God, the strength of the Holy Spirit.

Therefore, let us ask the Lord today to give us wonder before him, before the many spiritual treasures he has given us, and with this wonder that he give us joy, the joy of our lives and of living amid many difficulties with peace in our hearts. May he protect us from seeking happiness in the many things that ultimately make us sad, things that promise much, but will not give us anything. Remember this: a Christian is a man or woman of joy, of joy in the Lord; a man or woman of wonder.

## The Three Gazes of Jesus (10:17–30)[12]

The first scene presents the encounter between the Teacher and a fellow who—according to the parallel passage of Matthew—

is identified as a "young man." It is the encounter of Jesus with a young man. This man runs up to Jesus, kneels, and calls him "Good Teacher." Then he asks: "What must I do to inherit eternal life?" in other words, happiness (v. 17). "Eternal life" is not only the afterlife, but is a full life, fulfilled, without limitations. What must we do to achieve it? Jesus's answer restates the commandments that refer to loving one's neighbor. In this regard, the young man is beyond reproach. But clearly, observing the precepts is not enough. It does not satisfy his desire for fulfillment. Jesus perceives the desire in the young man's heart; for this reason his response is expressed in an intense gaze filled with tenderness and love. The Gospel thus says: "[Jesus] looking upon him loved him" (v. 21). He realized he was a good young man.... But Jesus also understood the young man's weakness, and he offered him a practical proposal: to give all his possessions to the poor and follow him. The young man's heart, however, was divided between two masters: God and money, and he went away sorrowful. This shows that faith and attachment to riches cannot coexist. Thus, in the end, the young man's initial enthusiasm waned.

In the second scene, the evangelist again mentions Jesus's gaze, and this time it is a pensive gaze, one of caution: "[Jesus] looked around and said to his disciples: 'How hard it will be for those who have riches to enter the kingdom of God!'" (v. 23). To the astonishment of the disciples, who ask him: "Then who can be saved?" (v. 26), Jesus responds with an encouraging gaze—the third gaze—and says: salvation, yes, "with men it is impossible, but not with God!" (v. 27). If we trust in the Lord, we can overcome all obstacles that impede us from following him on the path of faith. Trust in the Lord. He will give us strength; he gives us salvation, and he accompanies us on the way.

And thus we arrive at the third scene, that of Jesus's solemn declaration: "Truly, I say to you, those who leave all to follow me shall have eternal life in the age to come and a hundredfold now in this time" (cf. vv. 29–30). This "hundredfold" comprises things first possessed and then left, but that shall be restored and multiplied ad infinitum. In divesting oneself of possessions one receives in exchange the comfort of true good. Freed from the slavery of things, one earns the freedom of serving out of love; in renouncing possessions, one acquires the joy of giving. As Jesus said: "It is more blessed to give than to receive" (cf. Acts 20:35).

The young man did not allow himself to be conquered by Jesus's loving gaze, and thus was not able to change. Only by accepting with humble gratitude the love of the Lord do we free ourselves from the seduction of idols and the blindness of our illusions. Money, pleasure, and success dazzle but then disappoint; they promise life but procure death. The Lord asks us to detach ourselves from these false riches in order to enter into true life, into full, authentic, luminous life. I ask you, young people, young men and young women, who are here now in Saint Peter's Square: "Have you felt Jesus's gaze upon you? Do you prefer to leave this square with the joy that Jesus gives us or with the sadness of heart that worldliness offers us?"

## To Look with the Eyes of God (10:21, 51)[13]

It is a profound spiritual experience to contemplate our loved ones with the eyes of God and to see Christ in them. This demands a freedom and openness that enable us to appreciate their dignity. We can be fully present to others only by giving fully of ourselves and forgetting all else. Our loved ones merit our complete attention. Jesus is our model in this, for whenever people approached to speak with him, he would meet their gaze, directly and lovingly (cf. Mark 10:21). No one felt overlooked in his presence, since his words and gestures conveyed the question: "What do you want me to do for you?" (Mark 10:51). This is what we experience in the daily life of the family. We are constantly reminded that each of those who live with us merits complete attention, since he or she possesses infinite dignity as an object of the Father's immense love. This gives rise to a tenderness that can "stir in the other the joy of being loved. Tenderness is expressed in a particular way by exercising loving care in treating the limitations of the other, especially when they are evident."[14]

## An Attitude of Heart (10:21)[15]

We are speaking of an attitude of the heart, one that approaches life with serene attentiveness, that is capable of being fully present to someone without thinking of what comes next, that accepts each moment as a gift from God to be lived to the full. Jesus taught us this attitude when he invited us to contemplate the lilies of the field and the birds of the air, or when seeing the rich young man and knowing his restlessness, "he looked at him with love" (Mark 10:21). He was completely present to everyone and to everything, and in this way he showed us the way to overcome that unhealthy anxiety which makes us superficial, aggressive, and compulsive consumers.

## Our Wage from Jesus (10:28–31)[16]

When a Christian is attached to possessions, he gives the bad impression of a Christian who wants to have two things: heaven and earth. And the touchstone is exactly what Jesus says: the cross and persecutions imply self-denial and enduring the cross every day.

For their part, the disciples had this temptation: to follow Jesus, but wondering how this good deal would turn out. Let's consider James and John's mother, when she asked Jesus for a position for her sons: "Ah, make this one prime minister for me, that one the minister of finance." There was worldly interest in following Jesus. But then, the heart of these disciples was being purified, purified, purified until Pentecost, when they understood everything.

Gratuitousness in following Jesus is the response to the gratuitous love and the salvation that Jesus gives us. When one wants to follow both Jesus and the world, both poverty and wealth, the outcome is "halfway Christianity," which seeks material gain; it is the spirit of worldliness. And that Christian, in the words of the Prophet Elijah, "limps on two legs" because he doesn't know what he wants.

### *The key to understanding*

The key to understanding this discourse of Jesus is the last phrase: "Many who are first will be last, and the last will be first" (v. 31). In other words, one who believes himself to be, or who is the greatest among you, makes himself the servant: the smallest.

Following Jesus from a worldly perspective is not a good deal: it means service. After all, that is exactly what the Lord did, and if the Lord gives you the chance to be first, you must behave as the last, that is, by serving. And if the Lord gives you the chance to have possessions, you must place them in service, that is, service for others.

There are three things, three steps that separate us from Jesus: wealth, vanity, and pride. This is why possessions are so dangerous: they lead us immediately to vanity, and we believe we are important; and when we believe we are important, our head swells and we become lost. This is the reason that Jesus reminds us of the path: "Many who are first will be last, and he who is first among you will make himself the servant of all." It is a path of divesting, the same path that Jesus took.

For Jesus, this work of catechesis to the disciples took a really great deal of time, because they didn't understand well. Today we too must ask him: teach us this path, this way of service, this way of humility, this way of being last in order to serve our brothers and sisters. . . .

It is unseemly to see a Christian—whether lay or consecrated, priest or bishop—who wants both things: to follow Jesus and possessions, to follow Jesus and worldliness. It offers counter-testimony that separates people from Jesus. Let us continue to reflect on Peter's question: "We have left everything; how are you going to pay us?" And remember well Jesus's response, because the payment he will give us is likeness to him: this will be our "payment." And likeness to Jesus is a "great payment."

## THE COMMITMENT (10:17–31)[17]

"We have left everything and followed you" (10:28). Jesus's answer is clear: "I say to you, there is no one who has left everything who has not also received everything." In other words, there is no middle ground: "We have left everything"—"You will receive everything." There is, however, that overflowing measure with which God gives his gifts: "You will receive everything. There is no one who has left house or brothers or sisters or mother or father or children or lands, for my sake and for the Gospel, who will not receive a hundredfold now in this time, houses and brothers and sisters and mothers and children and lands with persecutions, and in the age to come eternal life. Everything."

This answer, however, contains a word that calls us to reflect. In fact, Jesus confirms that in our times, we already receive one hundred times more houses and brothers, together with persecution. Hence, everything and nothing. All with the cross, all with persecution. It requires a new way of thinking, a different way of behaving. In fact, Jesus gives all of himself, because the fullness, God's fullness, is a fullness that is forsaken with the cross. Here, then, is God's gift: a fullness that is forsaken, and here, too, is also the Christian way: to seek fullness, to receive this forsaken fullness, and to follow that path, which is a commitment that is not easy.

What is the sign, the signal that I am moving forward in this "giving everything" and "receiving everything"? In other words, what shows us that we are on the right path? The answer can be found in today's first reading (Sir 35:1–15), which says: "Glorify the Lord generously, and do not stint the first fruits of your hands. With every gift show a cheerful face, and dedicate your tithe with gladness. Give to the Most High as he has given, and as generously as your hand has found." Therefore, a "generous outlook, a cheerful face, joy": the sign that we are on the "everything and nothing" path of the forsaken fullness is joy. It is no surprise that the rich young man's countenance darkened and he went away saddened. He had not been able to receive this forsaken fullness. Instead, the saints, Peter himself, did receive this. And amid their trials and difficulties they had a cheerful face, a generous outlook, and joy in their hearts. This is the sign.

## The Way of the Cross (10:32)[18]

"Jesus was walking ahead of them . . ." (Mark 10:32). At this moment, too, Jesus is walking ahead of us. He is always before us. He goes ahead of us and leads the way. This is the source of our confidence and our joy: to be his disciples, to remain with him, to walk behind him, to follow him. . . .

And this is not easy, or comfortable, because the way that Jesus chooses is the way of the cross. As they journey together, he speaks to his disciples about what will happen in Jerusalem: he foretells his passion, death, and resurrection. And they are "shocked" and "full of fear." They are shocked, certainly, because for them going up to Jerusalem has meant sharing in the triumph of the Messiah, in his victory—we see this in the request made by James and John. But they are also full of fear of what is about to happen to Jesus, and of what they themselves might have to endure.

Unlike the disciples in those days, we know that Jesus has won, and that we need not fear the cross; indeed, the cross is our hope. And yet, we are all too human, sinners, tempted to think as men do, not as God does.

## The Way of Love (10:35–45)[19]

Today's gospel passage describes Jesus who, once again and with great patience, tries to correct his disciples, converting them from the world's mentality to that of God. The opportunity is given to him by the brothers James and John, two of the very first whom Jesus met and called to follow him. By now they have gone quite a long way with him and in fact belong to the group of the twelve apostles. Therefore, while they are on their way to Jerusalem—where the disciples anxiously hope that on the occasion of the celebration of Passover, Jesus will at last establish the kingdom of God—the two brothers take courage, approach the Teacher, and make their request: "Grant us to sit, one at your right hand and one at your left, in your glory" (v. 37).

Jesus knows that James and John are inspired by great enthusiasm for him and for the cause of the kingdom, but he also knows that their expectations and their zeal are tarnished by the spirit of the world. Thus he responds: "You do not know what you are asking" (v. 38). And as they are speaking of "thrones of glory" on which to sit beside Christ the King, he speaks of a "cup" to be drunk, of a "baptism" to be received, that is, his passion and death. James and John, always aiming at the hoped-for privilege, say in an outburst: yes, "We are able!" (v. 39). But here too, they do not truly understand what they are saying. Jesus forewarns that they will drink his cup and receive his baptism, that is, that they too, like the other apostles, will take part in his cross, when their time comes. However, Jesus concludes: "To sit at my right hand or at my left is not mine to grant, but it is for those for whom it has been prepared" (v. 40). As if to say: now follow me and learn how to love "at a loss," and the heavenly Father will see to your reward. The way of love is always "at a loss," because to love means to set aside egoism, self-referentiality, in order to serve others.

Jesus then realizes that the other ten apostles are angry with James and John, thus showing they have the same worldly mentality. And this offers him inspiration for a lesson that applies to Christians of all times, and for us too. He says: "You know that among the Gentiles those whom they recognize as their rulers lord it over them, and their great ones are tyrants over them. But it shall not be so among you; whoever wishes to become great among you must be your servant, and whoever wishes to be first among you must be slave of all" (vv. 42–44). It is the rule of Christians. The Teacher's message is clear: while the great people of the Earth build themselves "thrones" for their own power, God chooses an uncomfortable throne, the cross, from which to reign by giving his life: "The Son of man," Jesus says, "also came not to be served but to serve, and to give his life as a ransom for many" (v. 45).

The way of service is the most effective antidote against the disease of seeking first place; it is the medicine for status seekers, this seeking first place, which infects many and does not even spare Christians, the people of God, or even the ecclesiastical hierarchy. Therefore, as disciples of Christ, let us receive this call to conversion in order to witness with courage and generosity to a Church that bows at the feet of the least, in order to serve them with love and simplicity.

## Proclaim and Serve (10:45)[20]

The Lord was the first to show us this. He, the Word of the Father, who brought us the good news (cf. Isa 61:1), indeed, who is the good news (cf. Luke 4:18), became our servant (Phil 2:7). He came "not to be served, but to serve" (Mark 10:45). "He became the servant (*diakonos*) of all," wrote one of the Church Fathers (Saint Polycarp, *Ad Phil.* V, 2). We who proclaim him are called to act as he did. A disciple of Jesus cannot take a road other than that of the Master. If he wants to proclaim him, he must imitate him. Like Paul, *he must strive to become a servant.* In other words, if *evangelizing* is the mission entrusted at baptism to each Christian, *serving* is the way that mission is carried out. It is the only way to be a disciple of Jesus. His witnesses are those who do as he did: those who serve their brothers and sisters, never tiring of following Christ in his humility, never wearying of the Christian life, which is a *life of service.*

### *Availability*

How do we become "good and faithful servants" (cf. Matt 25:21)? First, we are asked to be *available*. A servant daily learns to detach himself from doing everything in his own way and living his life as he chooses. Each morning he trains himself to be generous with his life and to realize that the rest of the day will not be his own but will be given over to others. One who serves cannot hoard his free time; he has to give up the idea of being the master of his day. He knows that his time is not his own but a gift from God, which is then offered back to him. Only in this way will it bear fruit. One who serves is not a slave to his own agenda, but ever ready to deal with the unexpected, ever available to his brothers and sisters and ever open to God's constant surprises. One who serves is open to surprises, to God's constant surprises. A servant knows how to open the doors of his time and inner space for those around him, including those who knock on those doors at odd hours, even if it entails setting aside something he likes to do or giving up some well-deserved rest. One who serves is not worried about the timetable. . . .

The Gospel also speaks to us of service. It shows us two servants who have much to teach us: the servant of the centurion whom Jesus cures and the centurion himself, who serves the emperor. The words used by the centurion to dissuade Jesus from coming to his house are remarkable, and often the very opposite of our own: "Lord, do not trouble yourself, for I am not worthy to have you come under my roof" (Luke 7:6); therefore I did not presume to come to you" (v. 7); "I also am a man set under authority" (v. 8). Jesus marvels at these words. He is struck by the centurion's great humility, by his meekness. And meekness is one of the virtues of deacons. When a deacon is meek, then he is one who serves, who is not trying to "mimic" priests; no, he is meek. Given his troubles, the centurion might have been anxious and could have demanded to be heard, making his authority felt. He could have insisted and even forced Jesus to come to his house. Instead, he was modest, unassuming, and meek; he did not raise his voice or make a fuss. He acted, perhaps without even being aware of it, like God himself, who is "meek and humble of heart" (Matt 11:29). For God, who is love, is ever ready to serve us out of love. He is patient, kind, and always there for us; he suffers for our mistakes and seeks the way to help us improve. These are the characteristics of Christian service, meekness, and humility. *We imitate God by serving others*, by welcoming them with patient love and unflagging sympathy, by making them feel welcome and at home in the ecclesial community, where the greatest are not those who command but those who serve (cf. Luke 22:26)....

Each of us is very dear to God who loves us, chooses us, and calls us to serve. Yet each of us needs first to be healed inwardly. To be ready to serve, we need a healthy heart, a heart healed by God, a heart that knows forgiveness and is neither closed nor hardened. We would do well each day to pray trustingly for this, asking to be healed by Jesus, to grow more like him who "no longer calls us servants but friends" (cf. John 15:15).

## Your Faith Has Saved You (10:46–52)[21]

As the people of Israel were freed thanks to God's fatherhood, so too Bartimaeus is freed thanks to Jesus's compassion. Jesus has just left Jericho. Even though he has begun his most important journey, which will take him to Jerusalem, he still stops to respond to Bartimaeus's cry. Jesus is moved by his request and becomes involved in his situation. He is not content to simply offer him alms, but rather wants to personally encounter him. He does not give him any instruction or response, but asks him: "What do you want me to do for you?" (Mark 10:51). It might seem a senseless question: What could a blind man wish for if not his sight? Yet, with this question made face-to-face, directly but respectfully, Jesus shows that he wants to hear our needs. He wants to talk with each of us about our lives, our real situations, so that nothing is kept from him. After Bartimaeus's healing, the Lord tells him: "Your faith has made you well" (v. 52). It is beautiful to see how Christ admires Bartimaeus's faith, how he has confidence in him. He believes in us more than we believe in ourselves.

There is an interesting detail. Jesus asks his disciples to go and call Bartimaeus. They address the blind man with two expressions, which only Jesus uses in the rest of the Gospel. First they say to him: "Take heart!" which literally means, "Have faith, strong courage!" Indeed, only an encounter with Jesus gives a person the strength to face the most difficult situations. The second expression is "Rise!" as Jesus said to so many of the sick whom he took by the hand and healed. His disciples do nothing other than repeat Jesus's encouraging and liberating words, leading Bartimaeus directly to Jesus, without lecturing him. Jesus's disciples are called to this, even today, especially today: to bring people into contact with the compassionate Mercy that saves. When humanity's cry, like that of Bartimaeus, becomes stronger still, there is no other response than to make Jesus's words our own and, above all, imitate his heart. Moments of suffering and conflict are for God occasions of mercy. Today is a time of mercy!

There are, however, some temptations for those who follow Jesus. Today's Gospel shows at least two of them. None of the disciples stopped, as Jesus did. They continued to walk, going on as if nothing were happening. If Bartimaeus was blind, they were deaf: his problem was not their problem. This can be a danger for us. In the face of constant problems, we often feel it is better to move on, instead of letting ourselves be bothered. In this way, just like the disciples, we are with Jesus but we do not think like him. We are in his group, but our hearts are not open. We lose wonder, gratitude, and enthusiasm and we risk becoming habitually unmoved by grace. We are able to speak about him and work for him, but we live far from his heart, which is reaching out to those who are wounded. This is the temptation: a "spirituality of illusion." We can walk through the deserts of humanity without seeing what is really there; instead, we see what we want to see. We are capable of developing views of the world, but we do not accept what the Lord places before our eyes. A faith that does not know how to root itself in the life of people remains arid and, rather than creating oases, creates other deserts.

There is a second temptation, that of falling into a "scheduled faith." We are able to walk with the people of God, but we already have our schedule for the journey, where everything is listed: we know where to go and how long it will take; everyone must respect our rhythm and every problem is a bother. We run the risk of becoming the "many" of the Gospel who lose patience and rebuke Bartimaeus. Just a short time earlier, they scolded the children (cf. 10:13), and now the blind beggar: whoever bothers us or is not of our position in life is excluded. Jesus, however, wants to include, above all those kept on the fringes who are crying out to him. They, like Bartimaeus, have faith, because awareness of the need for salvation is the best way of encountering Jesus.

In the end, Bartimaeus follows Jesus on his path (cf. v. 52). He not only regains his sight but he joins the community of those who walk with Jesus. Dear Synod Fathers, we have walked together. Thank you for the path we have shared with our eyes fixed on Jesus and our brothers and sisters in the search for the paths which the Gospel indicates for our times so that we can proclaim the mystery of family love. Let us follow the path that the Lord desires. Let us ask him to turn to us with his healing and saving gaze, which knows how to radiate light as it recalls the splendor which illuminates it. Never allowing ourselves to be tarnished by pessimism or sin, let us seek and look upon the glory of God, which shines forth in men and women who are fully alive.

## What Kind of Christian Are We? (10:46–52)[22]

Jesus went with his disciples and with the people who followed him because he spoke like a master, with real authority. Bartimaeus, a blind man, heard the noise and asked, "What's happening?" It was Jesus. Then Bartimaeus began to cry out, and, in an act of faith, he cried out loudly, "Jesus, Son of David, have mercy on me!" His words were truly an act of faith.

Among the people who were there with Jesus, each one had his or her own personality, his or her own way of seeing life, of feeling life. First, there was a group of people who didn't hear the cry of the blind man. It is such people who, even today, don't hear the cry of the many who are in need of Jesus. In short, it is a group of people who are *indifferent*; they don't hear, and they believe that life is their own little group; they are happy, but they are deaf to the clamor of so many people in need of salvation, in need of Jesus's help, in need of the Church. These are selfish people; they live for themselves, unable to hear the voice of Jesus.

Then there are those who hear this cry for help, but *they want to silence it*. In fact, in the Gospel, Mark indicates that many people rebuked Bartimaeus to silence him, telling him not to cry out, to leave the Master in peace. Indeed, *even the disciples* do so. They keep the children away as well, so they won't disturb the Master. The disciples also tried to silence Bartimaeus, because the Master was their own, He was for them, not for everyone. In so doing, these people keep Jesus separate from those who cry out, who are in need of faith, who need salvation.

Some people were *businessmen*, who were religious, it seems, but Jesus cast them out of the temple because they were doing business there, in the house of God. These are people who don't hear—don't want to hear—the cry for help, but prefer to conduct their business and use the people of God, use the Church, to conduct their business. These businessmen too distance the people of Jesus and do not allow the people to ask for help.

Those who *push away the people of Jesus* are those who are Christians in name only, without witness, without bearing witness as Christians. Yes, they are Christians in name, showroom

Christians, holiday Christians, but their inner life is not Christian; it's worldly. Those who call themselves Christians but live as socialites distance those who cry out "Help!" to Jesus.

Then there are the *rigorists,* those whom Jesus rebukes because they lay such heavy burdens on people's shoulders. Jesus dedicates all of chapter 23 of Saint Matthew's Gospel to this group. He says to them: "Hypocrites, you exploit people!" In fact, instead of responding to the cry for salvation, they push the people away.

The first group comprises those who do not hear. The second includes many different, diverse types of people who hear the call but separate people from Jesus. Finally, there is a third group, those who help others to approach Jesus and who say to Bartimaeus: "Be brave, get up, he's calling you!" This is the group of Christians who are consistent: what they believe is what they live. It is the group of Christians who help those who cry out asking for salvation, asking for grace, asking for spiritual health for their soul, helping them to get close to Jesus.

Some questions for us: Which group am I in? In the first, with those who don't hear the many cries asking for the help of salvation? Am I closed, selfish, concerned with only my relationship with Jesus? Do I belong to the second group, those who separate people from Jesus whether by lacking coherence in life, failing to witness, being too attached to money, or being rigid? Do I distance people from Jesus? Or do I belong to the third group, with those who hear the cry of so many people and help them to approach Jesus? These are questions that each of us must answer in our hearts.

## Feeling Compassion (10:47–48)[23]

The piety that we wish to talk about is a manifestation of God's mercy. It is one of the seven gifts of the Holy Spirit, whom the

Lord offers to his disciples to render them "docile in readily obeying divine inspirations" (*Catechism of the Catholic Church*, n. 1831). Many times the Gospel refers to the spontaneous cry that the sick, those who are possessed, the poor, or afflicted people addressed to Jesus: "Have mercy" (cf. Mark 10:47–48; Matt 15:22; 17:15). Jesus responded to all with his gaze of mercy and the comfort of his presence. In those invocations for help or requests for mercy, each person also expressed his or her faith in Jesus, calling him "Teacher," "Son of David," and "Lord." They perceived that there was something extraordinary about him that could help them to emerge from their state of distress. They perceived in him the love of God himself. Even if the people were crowding around him, Jesus was aware of those cries for mercy and he was moved to compassion, especially when he saw people suffering and wounded in their dignity, as in the case of the hemorrhaging woman (cf. Mark 5:32). He called her to trust in him and in his word (cf. John 6:48–55). For Jesus, feeling compassion is the same as sharing in the distress of those he meets, but at the same time, it is also getting involved in a personal way so that their distress might be transformed into joy.

## 11
# Jerusalem

### Jesus Enters Jerusalem (11:1–14)[1]

The liturgy invites us to share in the joy and celebration of the people who cry out in praise of their Lord, a joy that will fade and leave a bitter and sorrowful taste by the end of the account of the passion. This celebration seems to combine stories of joy and suffering, mistakes and successes, which are part of our daily lives as disciples. It somehow expresses the contradictory feelings that we too, the men and women of today, experience: the capacity for great love... but also for great hatred; the capacity for courageous self-sacrifice, but also the ability to "wash our hands" at an opportune moment; the capacity for loyalty, but also for great abandonment and betrayal.

We also see clearly throughout the gospel account that the joy Jesus awakens is, for some, a source of anger and irritation.

Jesus enters the city surrounded by his people and by a cacophony of singing and shouting. We can imagine amid the outcry we hear, at the same time... the cry of those living on the edges of the city. And the cry of those men and women who followed Jesus because they felt his compassion for their pain and misery. . . . That outcry is the song and the spontaneous joy of all those left behind and overlooked, who, having been touched by Jesus, can now shout: "Blessed is the one who comes in the name of the Lord." How could they not praise the one who had restored their dignity and hope? Theirs is the joy of so many forgiven sinners who are able to trust and hope once again. And they cry out. They rejoice. This is joy.

All this joy and praise are a source of unease, scandal, and upset for those who consider themselves righteous and "faithful" to the law and its ritual precepts. A joy unbearable for those hardened against pain, suffering, and misery. Many of these think to themselves: "Such ill-mannered people!" A joy intolerable for those who have forgotten the many chances they themselves have been given. How hard it is for the comfortable and the self-righteous to understand the joy and the celebration of God's mercy! How hard it is for those who trust only in themselves and look down on others to share in this joy.

And so here is where another kind of shouting comes from, the fierce cry of those who shout out: "Crucify him!" It is not spontaneous but already armed with disparagement, slander, and false witness. It is a cry that emerges in moving from the facts to an account of the facts; it comes from this "story." It is the voice of those who twist reality and invent stories for their own benefit, without concern for the good name of others. This is a false account: the cry of those who have no problem in seeking ways to gain power and to silence dissonant voices; the cry that comes from "spinning" facts and painting them in such a way that they disfigure the face of Jesus and turn him into a "criminal"; the cry of those who want to defend their own position, especially by discrediting the defenseless; the cry born of the show of self-sufficiency, pride, and arrogance that sees no problem in shouting: "Crucify him, crucify him."

And so the celebration of the people ends up being stifled. Hope is demolished, dreams are killed, joy is suppressed; the heart is shielded and charity grows cold. It is a cry of "save yourself," which would dull our sense of solidarity, dampen our ideals, and blur our vision... the cry that wants to erase compassion, that "suffering with" that is compassion, and that is the weakness of God.

## Three Lifestyles (11:11–25)[2]

The gospel passage presents three attitudes linked to figures: those "of the fig tree," the "businessmen in the temple," and "the person of faith." These correspond to the three types of disciples of Jesus who were presented in the last chapter: those who don't hear the cry for help of the blind man; those who push people away from Jesus; and, last, those who help the people in need to go to Jesus.

The fig tree represents infertility, in other words, a barren life, incapable of giving anything because that type of person lives for himself, remains undisturbed and selfish, and doesn't want problems. In the gospel passage, Jesus curses the fig tree for being infertile because it made no effort to bear fruit. Therefore, it symbolizes the person who does nothing to help, who lives only for self and so wants for nothing.

Such people become neurotic in the end. And Jesus condemns the spiritual barrenness, the spiritual selfishness of those who think: "I live for myself, so I never want for anything. Let the others make do for themselves!"

Then there is a second lifestyle, which is that of those who exploit, like the unscrupulous businessmen in the temple. They even exploit the sacred place of God by conducting business there: they change coins; they sell sacrificial animals; they even have a sort of union among themselves for protection. Their lifestyle is not only tolerated but even permitted by the priests of the temple. For a clearer understanding of this, consider another really ugly scene from the Bible, which describes those who make a business of religion: the story of the priest whose sons urge the people to make offerings and so make a profit, even from the poor. Jesus spares no words for these men, and says to the merchants in the temple: "My house shall be called a house of prayer.... But you have made it a den of robbers." The people went to the temple on pilgrimage to ask the Lord's blessing, to make a sacrifice, and even there those people were exploited; the priests didn't teach them to pray, didn't provide catechesis.... It was a den of robbers. They didn't care whether there was true devotion: "You pay, you can enter!" They performed the rites without true devotion. I don't know if it would do us good to consider whether something like this happens with us in certain places, in other words, using the things of God for our own profit.

There is, finally, a third lifestyle, one that Jesus advises us to live, namely, the life of faith. When the disciples saw the fig tree shriveled to its roots because Jesus had cursed it, Peter said to him: "Master, look! The fig tree which you cursed has withered!" And Jesus, taking the opportunity to point out the just lifestyle, responded: "Have faith in God.... Whoever says to this mountain, 'Be taken up and cast into the sea,' and does not doubt in his heart, but believes that what he says will come to pass, it will be done for him.... Whatever you ask in prayer, believe that you will receive it, and you will." Therefore, what will come to pass is exactly what we ask with faith: it is the lifestyle of faith.

One could then ask: "Father, what must I do for this?" It is simple: ask the Lord, but with faith, that he may help you do good things. It is simple, but there is one condition, which is exactly what Jesus said: "Whenever you stand praying, forgive, if you have anything against any one. It is the only condition so that your Father who is in heaven may forgive you your trespasses." Thus, the third lifestyle is one that lives the faith so as to help others, to be closer to God; it is the faith that works miracles.

These are the three lifestyles presented to Christians: the first is that of barren persons who don't wish to bear fruit in life and who lead a comfortable, calm life without problems; it is the lifestyle of those who don't bother doing good. Then there are those who take advantage of others, even in the house of God: the exploiters, the unscrupulous businessmen of the temple, those whom Jesus drives out with a whip. And finally, there is the lifestyle of those who have trust in God, knowing that what they ask of the Lord with faith will come to pass. And this is precisely how Jesus advises us to live. The path of Jesus can be taken only on one condition: forgive, forgive others, so your Father may forgive you of so many things.

## SPEAKING WITH AUTHORITY (11:27–33)[3]

This gospel passage notes that "Jesus taught as one having authority." As Jesus preaches in the synagogue, the evangelist focuses on the reaction among the people to his way of acting with "authority," unlike the scribes. There is a difference between "having authority"—or the "inner authority" of Jesus—and the authority of the scribes who exercise it but "without having it." Despite being experts in teaching the law and being listened to by the people, they were not credible.

### *Jesus's authority*

The authority of the Lord is one of "lordship," with which he moved about, taught, healed, and heard the people. This lordship, from within, demonstrates the consistency between his teaching and his actions. It is this consistency, this testimony, that gives authority to a person. Hence, authority is seen in consistency and testimony.

### *Hypocritical pastors*

The scribes, on the other hand, were not consistent, which is why Jesus admonished the people to "do what they say but not what they do." Jesus also did not miss an opportunity to reproach the scribes because, with this attitude, they had fallen into a "pastoral schizophrenia"—saying one thing and doing something else. At times in the Gospels Jesus sometimes puts the scribes in a corner, does not give them any answers, or just describes them.

The word that Jesus uses to describe their inconsistency and schizophrenia is "hypocrisy." Such hypocrisy is the way of acting by those who have responsibility over the people, hence pastoral responsibility, but are not consistent. They are not lords and do not have authority, but the people of God are meek and tolerate many hypocritical and schizophrenic pastors who are not consistent, who say one thing but don't do it themselves.

### *An inconstant Christian*

The people of God, who are very tolerant, can recognize the power of grace. This is evident in the first reading from the Book of Samuel where the elderly priest, Eli had lost all authority, with only the grace of anointing remaining. With that grace, he blessed and performed the miracle for Anna, who, distraught by grief, was praying to be a mother. Reflecting on this scene, the people of God can distinguish well between a person's authority and the grace of anointing. They recognize a confessor after the heart of Christ. This is the wisdom of our people, who many times tolerate inconsistent pastors like the scribes and even Christians who go to Mass every Sunday and then live like pagans. People can easily recognize a scandal and inconsistent behavior. Inconstant Christians who don't give witness and inconsistent and schizophrenic pastors who don't give witness do much harm.

Let us pray that all baptized may have the "authority" that does not consist in commanding and making oneself heard but in being consistent, being a witness, and, in this way, being companions on the way of the Lord.

## 12
# Temple of Jerusalem

### Mercy and Conversion (12:1–11)[1]

What is conversion? The term is present throughout the Bible, and particularly in the preaching of the prophets who continually urge the people to "return to the Lord" by asking him for forgiveness and changing their ways. Conversion, according to the prophets, means changing direction and turning to the Lord anew, relying on the certainty that he loves us and his love is ever steadfast.

Jesus made conversion the first word of his preaching: "Repent and believe in the Gospel" (Mark 1:15). With this proclamation, he presents himself to the people, asking them to accept his words as God's final and definitive words to humanity (cf. Mark 12:1–11). Speaking of conversion with regard to the preaching of the prophets, Jesus insists even more on the interior dimension. In fact, conversion involves the whole person—heart and mind—to become a new creature, a new person. Change your heart and you will be renewed.....

How many times have we felt the need to effect a change that would involve our entire person! How often do we say to ourselves: "I need to change, I can't continue this way. . . . My life on this path will not bear fruit; it will be a useless life and I will not be happy." How often these thoughts come, how often! And Jesus, who is near us, extends his hand and says, "Come, come to me. I'll do the work: I'll change your heart; I'll change your life; I will make you happy." But do we believe this? Yes or no? What do you think: Do you believe this or not? Less applause and more voice! Do you believe or not? . . . Jesus who is with us invites us to change our life. It is he, with the Holy Spirit, who sows in us this restlessness to change our life and be better. Let us follow, therefore, this invitation of the Lord and let us not put up resistance, because only if we open ourselves to his mercy will we find true life and true joy.

All we have to do is open the door wide, and he will do the rest. He does everything, but we must open our heart wide so that he can heal us and allow us to go forward. I assure you that we will be much happier.

## Salvation from Rejection (12:1–12)[2]

The parable of the farmers and the master of the vineyard summarizes the history of salvation that Jesus delivered to the chief priests, the scribes, and the elders, that is, to the leaders of the people of Israel, to those who held the government of the people in their hands, to those who held the promise of God in their hands.

It's a beautiful parable, which begins with a dream, a project of love: a man plants a vineyard, sets a hedge around it, digs a pit for the wine press, and builds a tower. It is all done with love. Indeed, the man loves this seedling vineyard and therefore rents it out so that it may bear fruit. Then, when the time comes, he sends a servant to the farmers to collect his share of the harvest, and there begins all that we have heard: they club one servant, beat another, and kill another. Finally, he sends his son, but those farmers kill him, and that's how the story ends.

This story, which seemed like a love story, tracing the steps of love between God and his people, now appears instead to be a story of failures. At this point, God, the father of the people, who takes this people as they are, for they are a small people and they love him—they dream with love—seems to fail. Looked at like this, the history of salvation can well be called a history of failure. But the failure begins from the very first moment, for from the beginning of God's dream, there is blood—the blood of Abel—and from there it continues: the blood of all the prophets who went to speak to the people, to help protect the vineyard, up until the blood of his Son. However, in the end, there is God's word, which makes us think.

What, then, will the master of the vineyard do? "He will come and place his people before the judge." On this subject, Jesus says something that seems out of place: "Have you not read this scripture: 'The stone that the builders rejected has become the cornerstone; this was the Lord's doing, and it is amazing in our eyes'?" The history of failure turns around, and what was rejected becomes strength. And so the prophets, the men of God who spoke to the people, who weren't listened to, who were rejected, will be his glory. And the Son, the last one sent, who was truly cast out, judged, not listened to, and killed, will become the cornerstone. It is here, then, that the story that begins with a dream of love and appears to be a love story, then seems to result in a history of failures, ends with the great love of God who draws forth salvation out of the emptiness. His rejected Son saves us all.

Reading the many, many lamentations of God in the Bible is a beautiful experience. After all, when God speaks to his people he asks: "Why do you do this? Remember all that I have done for you, that I chose you; that I set you free. Why do you do this to me?" The Father laments, even weeps. And in the end there is Jesus weeping over Jerusalem: "Jerusalem, Jerusalem, which kills the prophets." This is the history of a people who cannot free themselves from that desire which Satan sowed in the first parents: you will become gods. It is a people who don't know how to obey God, because they want to become gods in their own right.

This attitude renders them a closed people, a people whose ministers are rigid. This is why the end of this passage is sad, because what emerges is the rigidity of those priests, of those doctors of the law: they try to capture Jesus in order to kill him but they are afraid of the crowd. In fact, they understand that he told that parable against them. And thus, they leave him and go away.

The path of our redemption is a road on which there is no shortage of failures. Indeed, even the last moment—the cross—is a scandal: but precisely there, love wins. And that history, which begins with a dream of love and continues with a history of failures, ends in the victory of love: the cross of Jesus. Do not forget this path, even though it is a difficult one. But ours, too, is always a difficult path. Thus, if each one of us examines his or her conscience, we will see how many times we have cast out the prophets; how many times we have said to Jesus: "Go away!"; how many times we have wanted to save ourselves; how many times we have wanted to be right.

The love of God for his people is manifest in the sacrifice of his Son who we will now celebrate once again, truly. When he descends upon the altar and we offer him to the Father, it will do us good to remember this story of love which seems to fail but wins in the end. Therefore, it is important to remember in the history of our life that seed of love which God has sown in us, and in response do what Jesus did on our behalf: he humbled himself. Thus, we too will do well to humble ourselves before this Lord who now comes to celebrate with us the remembrance of his victory.

## Prophecy, Memory, and Hope (12:1–12)[3]

It is clear to whom Jesus is speaking with this parable: to the chief priests, the scribes, and the elders of the people. For them, the Lord uses the image of a vineyard, which in the Bible represents the image of God's people, the image of the Church, and also the image of our soul. The Lord cares for the vineyard: he surrounds it; he digs a hole for the winepress; and he builds a tower.

It is precisely in this work that all of God's love and tenderness in making his people can be recognized: the Lord has always done this with so much love and tenderness. And he always reminds his people of the time when they were faithful, when they followed him in the desert, and when they searched for his face.

### *A people without memory*

However, the situation was then reversed. The people took hold of this gift from God, shouting: "It is us, we are free!" The people did not think, they did not remember that they were made by the hands and the heart of God, and in this way, they became a people without memory, a people without prophecy and without hope.

Therefore Jesus addresses the leaders of the people with this parable: a people without memory has forgotten the gift, and it attributes what it is to itself: we can! The Bible speaks many times of "ascetics and prophets," and Jesus himself emphasizes the importance of memory: a people who do not remember are not a people; they forget their roots, and they forget their history.

In the Book of Deuteronomy, Moses repeats this point several times: "You must remember, remember!" In fact, that is the book of the memory of the people, the people of Israel. It is the book of the Church's memory, but it is also the book of our personal memory. It is precisely this Deuteronomic dimension of life—the life of a people or of one person's life—that always returns to the roots in order to remember and to avoid making mistakes along the way. However, the people to whom Jesus addressed the parable had lost the memory. They had lost their memory of the gift, the gift of the God who had made them.

### *Without prophecy*

Having lost the memory, they are a people who are unable to make room for the prophets. Jesus himself tells them that they have killed the prophets, because the prophets encumber, the prophets always tell us what we do not want to hear. And so, Daniel complains in Babylon: "We, today, have no prophets!" These words contain the reality of a people with no prophets to indicate the way to them and remind them: the prophet is the one who takes the memory and helps people to move forward. That is why Jesus said to the leaders of the people: "You have lost your memory, and you do not have prophets. Or rather: when the prophets came, you killed them!"

### *Without hope*

Moreover, the attitude of the people's leaders was clear: "We have no need of prophets, we have ourselves!" But without memory or prophets, they become a people without hope, a people with no horizons, a people closed in on themselves who do not open up to the promises of God, who do not wait for God's promises. Therefore they are a people without memory, without prophecy, and without hope: these are the chief priests, the scribes, and the elders of the people of Israel.

And where is the faith? "In the crowd!" In the Gospel we read: "They tried to capture him, but they feared the crowd." The people in the crowd, in fact, understood the truth and, in the midst of their sins, they had memory, they were open to prophecy, and they sought hope. An example, in this respect, is seen in two elderly people, Simeon and Anna, people of memory, prophecy, and hope.

The leaders of the people legitimized their thoughts by surrounding themselves with lawyers, doctors of the law who used a legal system that was limiting, whose thinking was "closed and secure," whose attitude was: those who do this will be saved; the others do not interest us; memory does not interest us; it is better that the prophets not come. And hope? Well, that was up to each one. This is the system used to justify by the doctors of the law, the theologians who always choose the legal path and do not allow the freedom of the Holy Spirit; they do not recognize God's gift, the gift of the Spirit, and they put the Spirit in a cage, because they do not allow prophecy in hope. . . .

This lesson is for us too. We must ask ourselves: Do I remember the wonders that the Lord has done in my life? Do I remember the Lord's gifts? Am I capable of opening my heart to the prophets, to what they say to me: "This is wrong, you have to go there, move forward, take a risk," as the ancient prophets did? Am I open to that? Or am I afraid, preferring to lock myself in the cage of the law? And finally: Do I hope in God's promises, like our father Abraham did, who left his home without knowing where he was going, only because he hoped in God?

## The Hypocrites (12:13–17)[4]

In the gospel passage, Jesus uses the word "hypocrite" often to characterize the doctors of the law because he recognized their hypocrisy. They are hypocrites because they show one thing while they are thinking something else. Actually, according to the Greek etymology of the word, they speak, they judge, but underneath there is something else. Nothing could be more different from Jesus's way. Hypocrisy, in fact, is not the language of Jesus. Hypocrisy is not the language of Christians. This fact is absolutely clear!

However, as Jesus takes care to note, it is important that we fully understand hypocrisy and recognize how hypocrites behave.

Above all, the hypocrite is always a flatterer, whether to a greater or lesser degree, but he is a flatterer. Thus, for example, the doctors of the law say to Jesus: "Teacher, we know that you are true, and care for no man; for you do not regard the position of men, but truly teach the way of God." In other words, they use flattery to soften the other's heart and weaken resistance.

Therefore, hypocrites always begin with flattery. And then they ask a question. Part of flattery is not to speak the truth but rather to exaggerate, to boost vanity.... So, flattery always begins like this, but with an evil intention. This can be clearly seen in the gospel passage. In order to put Jesus to the test, the Pharisees fawned over him, so that he might believe them and slip up. This is the hypocrite's technique: he shows you that he likes you; he always puffs you up in order to achieve his aim.

Then there is a second aspect of what Jesus does when confronted with this two-faced ploy of the hypocrites who ask a fair question but with an unjust intention. They ask him: "Is it lawful to pay taxes to Caesar? Is it just?" Jesus, knowing their hypocrisy, states clearly: "Why put me to the test? Bring me a coin, and let me look at it." Observe Jesus's technique toward hypocrites and ideologues. Jesus always responds with reality. The reality is what it is; everything else is either hypocrisy or ideology.

This is why Jesus says: "Bring me a coin." He actually wants to show "reality." He responds "with wisdom": "Render to Caesar the things that are Caesar's"—the reality was that the coin bore the image of Caesar—"and to God the things that are God's."

### *The language of hypocrisy*

Finally, it is important to note a third aspect of the language of hypocrisy. It is a *language of deceit,* and it is the same language used by the serpent with Eve. It begins with flattery: "No . . . if you eat of this you will be great, you will know all . . ." in order to tempt her.

Hypocrisy, in fact, destroys. Hypocrisy kills. It kills people; it strips away a person's character and soul and it kills communities. When there are hypocrites in a community, there is a great danger. For this reason, the Lord Jesus said to us: "Let your speech be: yes, yes, no, no. Anything more comes from the evil one." He was very clear. In this regard, James, in his letter, was even stronger: "Let your yes be yes and your no be no."

These clear words help us understand today just how much evil hypocrisy does to the Church. So much evil is achieved by those Christians who fall into this sinful practice that kills! This is because the hypocrite is capable of killing a community. He speaks sweetly, while judging a person harshly. The hypocrite is a killer.

In conclusion, hypocrisy begins with flattery, to which one must respond only with reality, and hypocrisy uses the same language as the devil who sows his duplicitous language in communities in order to destroy them.

Let us ask the Lord to protect us from falling into the vice of hypocrisy, from masking our attitude that has evil intentions. Let us ask the Lord to give us this grace: "Lord, that I might never be a hypocrite, that I might know how to speak the truth, and if I cannot say it, to stay silent, but never to speak with hypocrisy."

## THE COMMANDMENT OF LOVE (12:28–34)[5]

At the heart of this gospel passage is the commandment of love: love of God and love of neighbor. A scribe asks Jesus: "Which commandment is the first of all?" (v. 28). He responds by quoting the profession of faith with which every Israelite opens and closes his day and begins with the words: "Hear O Israel: The Lord our God is one" (Deut 6:4). In this manner, Israel safeguards its faith in the fundamental reality of its whole creed: only one Lord exists and that Lord is "ours" in that he is bound to us by an indissoluble pact; he loved us, loves us, and will love us forever. It is from this source—this love of God—that the twofold commandment comes to us: "You shall love the Lord your God with all your heart, and with all your soul, and with all your mind, and with all your strength. . . . You shall love your neighbor as yourself" (Mark 12:30–31).

In choosing these two words addressed by God to his people and by putting them together, Jesus taught once and for all that love for God and love for neighbor are inseparable. Moreover, they sustain one another. Even if set in a sequence, they are two sides of a single coin; experienced together they are a believer's strength! To love God is to live of him and for him, for what he is and for what he does. Our God is unmitigated giving; he is unlimited forgiveness; he is a relationship that promotes and fosters. Therefore, to love God means to invest our energies each day to be his assistants in the unmitigated service of our neighbor, in trying to forgive without limitations, and in cultivating relationships of communion and fraternity.

Mark does not bother to specify who the neighbor is because a neighbor is a person whom I meet on the journey. It is not a matter of pre-selecting my neighbor; this is not Christian. My neighbor is not the one I have chosen ahead of time. No, this is not Christian; it is pagan. I discover my neighbor when I have eyes to see and a heart to want what is good for another person. If we practice seeing with Jesus's gaze, we will always be listening and close to those in need. Of course, our neighbor's needs require effective responses, but even beforehand, they require sharing. With one look, we can say that the hungry need not just a bowl of soup, but also a smile, to be listened to, and also a prayer, perhaps to be said together. Today's Gospel invites us all not only to be turned toward the needs of our poorest brothers and sisters but above all to be attentive to their need for fraternal closeness, for a meaning to life, and for tenderness. This challenges our Christian communities. It means avoiding the risk of being communities that have many initiatives but few relationships; the risk of being community "service stations" but with little company in the full and Christian sense of this term.

God, who is love, created us to love so that we can love others while remaining united with him. It would be misleading to claim to love our neighbor without loving God; and it would be deceptive to claim to love God without loving our neighbor. The two dimensions of love—God and neighbor—in their unity characterize the disciple of Christ.

## Two Types of Christian (12:38–41)[6]

This gospel passage is composed of two parts: one that describes *how not to be* followers of Christ; the other offers *an example* of a Christian.

### *How not to be a Christian*

Let's start with the first: what not to do. In the first part, Jesus accuses the scribes, the teachers of the law, of having three defects in their lifestyle: pride, greed, and hypocrisy. They like to be greeted in the marketplaces and to have the best seats in the synagogues and the places of honor at feasts (vv. 38–39). But beneath such solemn appearances they are hiding falsehood and injustice. While flaunting themselves in public, they use their authority—as Jesus says—to devour "the houses of widows" (cf. v. 40), those who, along with orphans and foreigners, were considered to be the most vulnerable and least protected people. Finally, Jesus says that the scribes, "for the sake of appearance say long prayers" (v. 40).

Even today, we risk taking on these attitudes, for example, when our prayer is separate from justice so that God cannot be worshiped, and when we cause harm to the poor, or when we claim to love God but instead offer him only grandiosity for the sake of our own advantage.

### *How to be a Christian*

The second part of the Gospel sets out how to be a Christian. The scene is set in the temple of Jerusalem, precisely in the place where people are depositing coins as offerings. There are many rich people putting in large sums, and there is a poor woman, a widow, who contributes only two small coins. Jesus observes the woman carefully and calls the disciples' attention to the sharp contrast in the scene.

The wealthy contributed with great ostentation what for them was superfluous, while the widow, Jesus says, "put in everything she had, her whole living" (v. 44). She gave the most of all. Because of her extreme poverty, she could have offered a single coin to the temple and kept the other for herself. But she did not want to give just half to God; she divested herself of everything. In her poverty, she understood that in having God, she had everything. She felt completely loved by him and in turn loved him completely. What a beautiful example this little old woman offers us!

Today, Jesus also tells us that the benchmark is not quantity but fullness of heart. There is a difference between quantity and fullness. You can have a lot of money and still be empty. There is no fullness in your heart. This week, think about the difference there is between quantity and fullness. It is not a matter of the wallet, but of the heart. There is a difference between the wallet and the heart.... There are diseases of the heart that reduce the heart to the wallet. . . . This is not good! To love God "with all your heart" means to trust in him, to trust in his providence, and to serve him in our poorest brothers and sisters without expecting anything in return.

Allow me to tell you a story of something that happened in my previous diocese. A mother and her three children were at the table. The father was at work. They were eating Milan-style cutlets. . . . There was a knock at the door and one of the children (they were young—five, six, and the oldest was seven) came and said: "Mom, there is a beggar asking for something to eat."

And the mother, a good Christian, asked them: "What shall we do?"

"Let's give him something, Mom."

"Okay." She took her fork and knife and cut the cutlets in half.

"Oh no, Mom, no! Not that! Get something from the fridge."

"No," she responded. "Let's make four sandwiches from what's left here!" The children learned that true charity is given, not with what is extra but with what we need. That afternoon I am sure that the children were a bit hungry. . . . But this is how it's done!

Faced with the needs of our neighbors, we are called—like these children with the halved cutlets—to deprive ourselves of essential things, not only of the superfluous. We are called to give the time that is necessary, not only what is extra; we are called to give immediately and unconditionally some of our talent, not what's left after having used it for our own purposes or for our own group.

Let us ask the Lord to admit us to the school of this poor widow whom Jesus presents as a teacher of the living Gospel even to the astonishment of the disciples. Through the intercession of Mary, let us ask for a heart that is poor but rich in glad and freely given generosity like that of the poor woman who gave her entire life to God.

## Quality over Quantity (12:38–44)[7]

Today's Gospel concludes the series of Jesus's teachings given in the temple of Jerusalem and highlights two contrasting figures: the scribe and the widow. But why are they contrasted? The scribe represents important, wealthy, influential people; the other person—the widow—represents the least, the poor, the weak. In reality, Jesus's resolute judgment of the scribes is not about the whole profession but refers to those of them who flaunt their own social position, embellish themselves with the title "Rabbi," that is, teacher, and love to be revered and take the best seats (cf. vv. 38–39).

What is worse is that their ostentation is, above all, of a religious nature because they pray and—Jesus says—"for the sake of appearance say long prayers" (v. 40) and use God in order to gain respect for themselves as the defenders of his law. This attitude of superiority and vanity causes them to have contempt for those who count for little or who, like widows, find themselves in an unfavorable economic position.

Jesus exposes this perverse mechanism. He denounces the oppression of the weak carried out misleadingly on the basis of religious motivations, and he declares clearly that God is on the side of the least. And to really impress this lesson on the minds of the disciples, he offers them a living example: a poor widow whose social position was irrelevant because she had no husband to defend her rights and therefore became easy prey to unscrupulous creditors who specialized in hounding the weak for payment. This woman goes to the temple treasury to put in just two coins—all that she had left—and she makes her offering by seeking to pass by unobserved, almost as if ashamed. But, in this very humility, she performs an act laden with great religious and spiritual significance. That gesture full of sacrifice does not escape the gaze of Jesus, who instead sees shining in it the total self-giving he wishes to teach his disciples.

The lesson that Jesus offers us today helps us to recover what is essential in our life and fosters a practical and daily relationship with God. Brothers and sisters, the Lord's scales are different from ours. He weighs people and their actions differently: God does not measure quantity but quality; he examines the heart; he looks at the purity of intention. This means that our "giving" to God in prayer and to others in charity should always steer clear of ritualism and formalism, as well as of the logic of calculation. It must be an expression of gratuity in imitation of Jesus who saved us freely. We must do things as an expression of gratuity. This is why Jesus points to that poor and generous widow as a model of Christian life. We do not know her name. However, we know her heart—we will find her in heaven and go to greet her, certainly; and that is what counts before God. When we are tempted by the desire to stand out and give an accounting of our altruistic gestures, when we are too interested in the gaze of others and—might I say—when we act like "peacocks," let us think of this woman. It will do us good. It will help us to divest ourselves of the superfluous in order to go to what truly counts, and to remain humble.

May the Virgin Mary, a poor woman who gave herself totally to God, sustain us in the aim of giving to the Lord and to our brothers and sisters not something of ours but instead ourselves, as a humble and generous offering.

13

# Being Prepared

## Persecution (13:9–13)[1]

The Church has been, is, and will always be persecuted. The Lord warned us of the danger (cf. Matt 24:4–14; Mark 13:9–13; Luke 21:12–19) so that we could be prepared. The Church will be oppressed and tyrannized, although not in her mediocre children who come to terms with the world, as did those renegades of which the book of the Maccabees speaks to us (cf. 1 Mac 1:11–15). It will be, however, in the other children, those who in the midst of a "multitude of witnesses" choose to keep their eyes fixed on Jesus (cf. Heb 12:1–2) and to follow in his footsteps at any cost. The Church will be persecuted insofar as it maintains its loyalty to the Gospel. The testimony of this absolute loyalty annoys the world, infuriates it, and makes it grind its teeth (cf. Acts 7:54), kill, and destroy, as happened with Stephen.

## The Coming of the Son of God (13:24–32)[2]

This gospel passage offers us part of Jesus's discourse regarding the final events of human history, oriented toward the complete fulfillment of the reign of God. It is the talk that Jesus gave in Jerusalem before his last Passover. It has certain apocalyptic elements, referring to things such as wars, famine, and cosmic catastrophes: "The sun will be darkened, and the moon will not give its light, and the stars will be falling from heaven, and the powers in the heavens will be shaken" (vv. 24–25). However, these aspects are not the essential part of the message. *The core around which Jesus's words turn is he himself*, the mystery of his person, of his death and resurrection and return at the end of time.

Our final goal is the encounter with the Risen Lord. I would like to ask: How many of us think about this? There will be a day on which I meet the Lord face to face. And this is our goal: the encounter. We do not await a time or a place, but we are going to encounter a person—Jesus. Thus the problem is not "when" these warning signs of the last days will occur, but rather whether we will be prepared. Neither is it about knowing "how" these things will happen, but instead "how" we have to act today in awaiting these things. We are called to live the present, building our future with serenity and trust in God.

### *The parable of the fig tree*

The parable of the fig tree that sprouts as a sign of the approaching summer (cf. vv. 28–29) teaches that the perspective of the end doesn't distract us from the present life but rather brings us to look at our current days with hope. This virtue of hope is so hard to live. It is the smallest but strongest of the virtues. And our hope has a face: the face of the Risen Lord, who comes "with great power and glory" (v. 26), which will manifest his love, crucified and transfigured in the resurrection. The triumph of Jesus at the end of time will be the triumph of the cross, the demonstration that the sacrifice of oneself for love of neighbor, in imitation of Christ, is the only victorious power, the only stable point amid the upheavals and tragedies of the world.

The Lord Jesus is not only the destination of our earthly pilgrimage but also a constant presence in our lives. He is beside us, and he always accompanies us. That is why, when we speak of the future and project ourselves toward it, it is always in order to lead us back to the present. Jesus counters the false prophets, the fortune-tellers who predict that the end of the world is near; he sets himself against fatalism. He is at our side. He walks with us, and he loves us. He wants to remove from his disciples of every age the curiosity about dates, predictions, and horoscopes and have them instead focus their attention on the today of history.

I would like to ask you: How many of you read your horoscope every day? When you feel like reading your horoscope, look rather to Jesus who is with you. This is better and will be better for you. The presence of Jesus calls us to the anticipation and vigilance that exclude both impatience and lethargy—both escaping to the future and becoming prisoners of the current moment and of worldliness.

In our days, too, there is no lack of natural and moral disaster, or of adversities and difficulties of every kind. Everything passes, the Lord reminds us, and he alone, his Word, remains as the light that guides and encourages our steps. He always forgives us because he is at our side. We need only look at him and he changes our hearts. We pray that the Virgin Mary may help us to trust in Jesus, the firm foundation of our life, and to persevere with joy in his love.

## Take Heed and Watch (13:33–37)[3]

In this gospel passage, Jesus exhorts us to take heed and watch so as to be ready to welcome him at the moment of his return. He tells us: "Take heed, watch . . . for you do not know when the time will come. . . . Watch therefore . . . lest he come suddenly and find you asleep" (vv. 33–37).

The person who takes heed is the one who, amid the worldly din, does not let himself or herself be overwhelmed by distraction or superficiality but lives in a full and conscious way, with concern first and foremost for others. In this manner we become aware of the tears and the needs of our neighbors, and we can also understand their human and spiritual strengths and qualities. The heedful person then also turns toward the world, seeking to counter the indifference and cruelty in it and taking delight in its beautiful treasures that are to be safeguarded. It is a matter of having an understanding gaze so as to recognize both the misery and poverty of individuals and of society as well as the richness hidden in the small, everyday things, precisely where the Lord has placed us.

The watchful person is the one who accepts the invitation to keep watch, that is, not to let oneself be overpowered by listlessness of discouragement, by lack of hope, by disappointment. At the same time keeping watch wards off the allure of the many vanities with which the world is brimming and for which, now and then, time as well as personal and familial peace are sacrificed. It is the painful experience of the people of Israel, recounted by the prophet Isaiah: God seemed to have let his people stray from his ways (cf. 63:17), but this was a result of the unfaithfulness of the people themselves (cf. 64:4b). Too often, we find ourselves in this situation of unfaithfulness to the call of the Lord. He shows us the good path, the way of faith, the way of love, but we seek our happiness elsewhere.

Being attentive and watchful are prerequisites for not continuing to "stray from the Lord's ways"—being lost in our sins and in our unfaithfulness. Being attentive and being watchful are the conditions that allow God to permeate our existence in order to restore meaning and value to it with his presence, full of goodness and tenderness.

Let us pray that Mary Most Holy, our role model for awaiting God and icon of watchfulness, may lead us to her son Jesus, rekindling our love for him.

# 14
# The Passion

## Respect and Gratitude (14:7)[1]

Respect and gratitude for the elderly must be witnessed to primarily by their families. The word of God urges us, in many ways, to respect and value older people and the elderly. It also invites us to learn from them, to be grateful to them, and to respect their solitude and fragility. Jesus's comment: "For you always have the poor with you, and you can show kindness to them whenever you wish; but you will not always have me" (v. 7), can be correctly applied to the elderly, because they are part of our family, people, and nation. However, they are too often forgotten or neglected by society and even by their own families.

Respect and gratitude are the virtuous, fundamental attitudes required to build a more just and fraternal society.

## The Passover (14:12–16, 22–26)[2]

The gospel passage speaks of the Last Supper, but surprisingly, it pays more attention to the preparations than to the dinner itself.

We keep hearing the word "prepare." For example, the disciples ask: "Where do you want us to go and prepare for you to eat the Passover?" (Mark 14:12). Jesus sends them off with clear instructions to make the necessary preparations, and they find "a large room . . . furnished and ready" (v. 15). The disciples go off to prepare, but the Lord has already made his own preparations.

Something similar occurs after the resurrection, when Jesus appears to the disciples for the third time. While they are fishing, he waits for them on the shore where he has already prepared bread and fish for them. Even so, he tells the disciples to bring some of the fish that they have just caught, the fish that he has shown them how to catch (cf. John 21:6, 9–10). Jesus has already made preparations, and he asks his disciples to cooperate. Once again, just before the Passover meal, Jesus tells the disciples: "I go to prepare a place for you . . . so that where I am, there you may be also" (John 14:2, 3). Jesus is the one who prepares, yet before his own Passover he also asks us urgently, with exhortations and parables, to be prepared, to remain ever ready (cf. Matt 24:44; Luke 12:40).

Jesus, then, prepares for us and asks us to be prepared. What does Jesus prepare for us? He prepares a place and a meal. The place he prepares for us is much more meaningful than the "large furnished room" of the Gospel. It is our spacious and vast home here below—the Church—where there is, and must be, room for everyone. But he has also reserved a place for us on high, in heaven, so that we can be with him and with one another forever. In addition to a place, he prepares a meal, the Bread in which he gives himself: "Take; this is my body" (Mark 14:22). These two gifts—a place and a meal—are what we need to live. They are our ultimate "room and board." Both are bestowed upon us in the Eucharist. A place and a meal.

Jesus prepares a place for us here below, and the Eucharist is the beating heart of the Church. It gives her birth and rebirth; it gathers her together and gives her strength. But the Eucharist also prepares for us a place on high, in eternity, for it is the Bread of heaven. It comes down from heaven—it is the only material on earth that has the taste of eternity. It is the bread of things to come. Even now it grants us a foretaste of a future infinitely greater than all we can hope for or imagine. It is the bread that sates our greatest expectations and feeds our finest dreams. It is, in a word, the pledge of eternal life—not simply a promise but a pledge, a concrete anticipation of what awaits us there. The Eucharist is our "reservation" for the heavenly banquet. It is Jesus himself as food for our journey toward eternal life and happiness.

In the consecrated host, in the place he has prepared for us, Jesus prepares for us a meal, food for our nourishment. In life, we constantly need to be fed, nourished not only with food but also with plans and affection, hopes and desires. We hunger to be loved. But the most pleasing compliments, the finest gifts, and the most advanced technologies are not enough; they never completely satisfy us. The Eucharist is simple food, like bread, yet it is the only food that satisfies, for there is no greater love. There we truly encounter Jesus. We share his life and we feel his love. There we can realize that his death and resurrection are for us. And when we worship Jesus in the Eucharist, we receive from him the Holy Spirit and we find peace and joy. Dear brothers and sisters, let us choose this food of life! Let us make Mass our priority! Let us rediscover eucharistic adoration in our communities! Let us ask for the grace to hunger for God with an insatiable desire to receive what he has prepared for us.

As he did with his disciples, so too Jesus asks us today to prepare. Like the disciples, let us ask him: "Lord, where do you want us to go to prepare?" Where: Jesus does not prefer exclusive, selective places. He looks for places untouched by love, untouched by hope. Those uncomfortable places are where he wants to go and he asks us to prepare his way. How many persons lack adequate housing or food to eat! All of us know people who are lonely, troubled, and in need; they are abandoned tabernacles. We, who receive from Jesus our own room and board, are here to prepare a place and a meal for these, our brothers and sisters in need. Jesus became bread broken for our sake. In turn, he asks us to give ourselves to others, to live no longer for ourselves but for one another. In this way, we live "eucharistically," pouring out upon the world the love we draw from the Lord's flesh. The Eucharist is translated into life when we pass it on beyond ourselves to those all around us.

The Gospel tells us that the disciples prepared for the meal after they "set out and went to the city" (v. 16). The Lord also calls us today to prepare for his coming not by separating ourselves but by entering our cities.... Lord, how many doors do you want us to open for you here? How many gates do you call us to unbar, how many walls must we tear down? Jesus wants the walls of indifference and silent collusion to be breached, iron bars of oppression and arrogance to be torn asunder, and paths cleared for justice, civility, and legality.... But this requires loosening the knots that keep us bound to the moorings of fear and depression. The Eucharist invites us to let ourselves be carried along by the wave of Jesus, to not remain grounded on the beach in the hope that something may come along, but to cast into the deep—free, courageous, and united.

The Gospel ends by telling us that the disciples, "after singing a hymn, went out" (v. 26). At the end of Mass, we too will go out. We will go forth with Jesus, who will pass through the streets of this city.

Jesus wants to dwell among you. He wants to be part of your lives, to enter your houses and to offer his liberating mercy, his blessing, and his consolation. You have experienced painful situations; the Lord wants to be close to you.

Let us open our doors to him and say:
Come, Lord, and visit us.

We welcome you into our hearts,
our families and our city.
We thank you because you have prepared for us
the food of life and a place in your kingdom.
Make us active in preparing your way,
joyous in bringing you, who are life, to others,
and thus bring fraternity, justice and peace
to our streets. Amen.

## Love and Forgiveness (14:22)[3]

The Gospel presents the narrative of the institution of the Eucharist performed by Jesus during the Last Supper in the upper room in Jerusalem. On the eve of his redeeming death on the cross, he fulfilled what had been foretold: "I am the living bread that came down from heaven; if any one eats of this bread, he will live forever; and the bread that I shall give for the life of the world is my flesh. . . . He who eats my flesh and drinks my blood abides in me, and I in him" (John 6:51, 56). Jesus takes the bread in his hands and says, "Take; this is my body" (Mark 14:22). With this gesture and with these words, he assigns to the bread a function which is no longer simply that of physical nutrition, but that of making his Person present in the midst of the community of believers.

The Last Supper represents the culmination of Christ's entire life. It is not only the anticipation of his sacrifice, which will be rendered on the cross, but also the synthesis of a life offered for the salvation of all humanity. Therefore, it is not enough to state that Jesus is present in the Eucharist; one must see in it the presence of a life given and partake in it. When we take and eat that Bread, we are invited into the life of Jesus, we enter into communion with him, we commit ourselves to achieving communion among ourselves, to transforming our life into a gift, especially for the poorest.

Today's feast evokes this message of solidarity and urges us to welcome the intimate invitation to conversion and to service, love, and forgiveness. It urges us to become, with our lives, imitators of that which we celebrate in the liturgy. Christ, who nourishes us under the consecrated species of bread and wine, is the same One who comes to us in everyday happenings. He is in the poor person who holds out his hand, in the suffering one who begs for help, in the brother or sister who asks for our availability and awaits our welcome. He is in the child who knows nothing about Jesus or salvation—who does not have faith. He is in every human being, even in the smallest and the most defenseless.

The Eucharist, source of love for the life of the Church, is the school of charity and solidarity. Those who are nourished by the Bread of Christ cannot remain indifferent to those who do not have their daily bread.

## ABANDONMENT (14:32–34)[4]

The silence of God coincides with the silence of men and the experience of exile itself. We are stripped of what we have, and we find ourselves "along the rivers of Babylon," where we hung up our harps, where we sat and wept, remembering Zion (cf. Ps 137:1).

The feeling of abandonment occurs at the height of the Lord's passion, in particular, in the prayer at Gethsemane which is one of the most human and dramatic entreaties of Jesus (cf. Mark 14:32–34; Matt 26:36–46; Luke 22:40–46). His prayer expresses the dimensions of exploration, sadness, and anguish that an exile suffers, far from the Lord.

The feeling of abandonment also reached a peak in the sadness of Jonah, who did not understand God's plans (cf. Gen 4:9). "My God, my God, why did you abandon me?" (Matt 27:46). The one who prays in such moments walks a path of purification. The heart is not at peace, but it strives to understand. The attitude, the words, the thoughts alternate in conflicting ways: one goes from tiredness to resignation (cf. Job 29:4), or slips into bitter irony (cf. Job 7:20), or looks for logical explanations (cf. Job 10:8), or assumes mistrustful attitudes (Job 10:2).

But beyond all this, the person who knows he is in exile remembers his homeland, lets the heart sigh, does not negotiate, does not go back, but takes a step forward and goes in search of God, beyond conventional shelters. He starts from his solitude, from his exile, from that silence he doesn't understand, from his world wounded by pain.

## ABBA! FATHER! (14:36)[5]

Christian prayer is personal. When we say "God," we usually mean the Father or Jesus, but there are also people who pray to God as if God were a divine abstraction. This is not prayer. Christian prayer is deeply personal, a face-to-face relationship: we turn to the Father, to the Son, or to the Holy Spirit. Let us also remember that each of the three persons of the Trinity has a different relationship with us in prayer.

It is worth repeating that it is God himself who inspires our prayer. The Holy Spirit suggests to us what the Father wants to hear. He "comes to the aid of our weakness," advising us as to what should be asked according to the divine design (cf. Rom 8:26–27).

### *Identifying with Christ*

It is necessary to remain united to Christ and, like Christ, be aware of being loved by the Father as the Father loves the Son (cf. John 16:27). And if the power of prayer lies precisely in abandoning oneself to the Spirit, praying means identifying with Christ. Christ is our door to the Father, to whom we turn with the words that Jesus taught us: "Abba! Father!" (Mark 14:36). The prayerful Christian cannot ignore this relationship. In prayer our flesh, identified with the flesh of the Word and guided by the Spirit, seeks the Father. This is the mystery that is revealed in prayer and that promises us communion with the Father, in the Spirit, through the Son (i.e., participation in this exchange of love; he takes our flesh, and we receive his Spirit).

## WATCHING (14:37–38)[6]

On the night of the beginning of the passion, the Lord said to Peter: "Simon, are you sleeping?" (Mark 14:37–38). The Lord wishes us to watch with him. . . .

### *The night of the exodus*

One of the strongest images . . . is that of the exodus from Egypt, where we are told that the Lord watched over his people on Passover night, called "the night of vigil": "That was for the Lord a night of vigil, to bring them out of the land of Egypt. That same night is a vigil to be kept for the Lord by all the Israelites throughout their generations" (Exod 12:42). . . .

Watching means patiently enduring the different ways in which the Lord continues to prepare for the salvation of his people. To watch, one must have meekness, patience, and the constancy of loving actions. . . . To watch, one needs to know the essentials. . . .

Watching speaks to us of hope: the hope of the merciful Father who watches over the progress of his children who are always close to his heart, letting them go their own way—of separation or fulfillment—and ready to prepare a party, so that, on their return home, they find the embrace and the loving dialogue they need.

# 15
# Crucifixion and Burial

## Jesus Was Silent (15:5)[1]

Silence is the highest and most common expression of dignity, especially in times of trial and crucifixion when the flesh would like to justify itself and escape the cross. In the supreme moment of injustice, "Jesus was silent" (Matt 26:63; cf. also Isa 53:7; Acts 8:32). He did not play the game of answering those who told him to come down from the cross. The eternal silence of the Word, the "contemplative" love of the Father and the Son and the Holy Spirit, all the Trinitarian communion from the silence of the centuries intrudes into the history of humanity. He is the Word, but the Word that, in the hour of annihilation caused by injustice, is silent. *Iesus autem tacebat*. (Jesus remains silent.) We contemplate the entire "journey" of the Word of God (cf. John 1:1; 14:2–3; 14:10; 16:28); we note the tenderness of a mother who "guarded all these things, meditating on them in her heart" (cf. Luke 2:19, 51). . . .

As an aside, the Gospel offers the following reflection. While proceeding on his way up toward Jerusalem, Jesus confides that he comes only to the apostles and not to all disciples. Certainly,

Jesus now hopes that every Christian will associate with this decisive event that took place in Jerusalem. But Jesus is the Lord of time and personal calling. He decides when he invites his disciples to take part in this privileged moment and go up with him to Jerusalem, toward the goal of that painful end.

## The Passion of Christ (15:16–20)[2]

***The cruelty...***

The saying, "Fallen trees make wood," relates precisely to the attitude of a criminal. There is an inherent cruelty deep within us that rebels against God and that shows itself when someone threatens us in our weakness. Jeremiah clearly denounces it: "But I was like a gentle lamb led to the slaughter. And I did not know it was against me that they devised schemes, saying 'Let us destroy the tree with its fruit, let us cut him off from the land of the living, so that his name will no longer be remembered!'" (Jer 11:19). The "songs of the suffering servant" (Isa 53:1ff.) describe this cruelty that was actualized in the passion of Christ.

***...continues even today***

On this point, there are two observations: First, people abuse those they consider weaker. Against Jesus they dared not do anything for fear of people (cf. Matt 26.5). They saw him as strong because everyone followed him and many believed in him (John 7:40–52; 10:42; 8:30). It was only when Jesus was "weakened" by the betrayal of one of his own (Matt 26:14–16) that they managed to come forward.

Second, at the root of all cruelty there is a need to unload one's faults and limitations. Jesus was a living reproach. Because of this he was made a scapegoat (cf. Lev 16:20–22). All evils are concentrated in the scapegoat.... Pontius Pilate "realized that it was out of jealousy that they had handed him over"

(Matt 27:18), and the crowd, swollen with the ranks of silent witnesses, through their silence became accomplices.

### Save Yourself! (15:29–32)[3]

Our faithfulness to the cross of Christ will undergo temptations. Sometimes, they will be like a whisper that is barely noticeable. At other times, they will confront us defiantly, but the phrase will always be the same: "He saved others; he cannot save himself. He is the King of Israel; let him come down from the cross now, and we will believe in him" (Matt 27:42–43). Our blindness to this temptation is all the stronger when our sinful hearts cling to other ways of life different from those which the Lord wants. Sometimes the Lord wills that we be harassed, like him, to the extreme of the cross—"If you are the Son of God, come down from the cross"—and we will not always have a companion who, in our situation, reminds us of the truth: "Do you not fear God, since you are under the same sentence of condemnation? And we indeed have been condemned justly, for we are getting what we deserve for our deeds, but this man has done nothing wrong" (Luke 23:40–41).

### The Power of the Cross (15:30–31)[4]

In the failure of the cross, one can see love—a love that is gratuitous, a love that Jesus gives us. For a Christian, speaking of power and strength means referring to the power of the cross and the strength of Jesus's love, a love that remains steadfast and complete even when faced with rejection; a love that is shown as the fulfillment of a life expended in the total surrender of oneself for the benefit of humanity. On Calvary, the passers-by and the leaders derided Jesus, nailed to the cross, and they challenged him: "Save yourself, and come down from the cross!" (Mark 15:30). "Save yourself!" But, paradoxically, the truth of Jesus is precisely what is hurled at him in a mocking tone by his adversaries: "He cannot save himself!" (v. 31). Had Jesus come down from the cross, he would have given in to the temptations of the prince of this world. Instead, he cannot save himself precisely so as to save others—because he has given his life for us, for each one of us. To say: "Jesus gave his life for the world" is true. But it is more beautiful to say: "Jesus gave his life for me." And today... let each one of us say in his or her heart: "He gave his life for me, in order to save each one of us from our sins."

### *The good thief*

Who understood this? One of the criminals who was crucified with him understood it well. The so-called good thief, implored him, "Jesus, remember me when you come into your kingdom" (Luke 23:42). But this was a criminal, a corrupt person, and he was there because he had been condemned to death for all of the brutalities that he had committed in his life. However, he saw love in Jesus's manner, in Jesus's meekness. The kingship of Jesus doesn't oppress us, but rather frees us from our weaknesses and miseries, encouraging us to walk the path of the good, of reconciliation and of forgiveness. Let us reflect on the cross of Jesus, let us reflect on the "good thief," and let us all say together what the good thief said: "Jesus, remember me when you come into your kingdom." Let us ask Jesus, when we feel weak, when we feel that we are sinners and defeated, to look at us. Let us say to him: "You are there. Don't forget me."

## Consolation and Strength (15:34)[5]

Christians know that suffering cannot be eliminated, yet it can have meaning and become an act of love and surrender into the hands of God who does not abandon us. In this way, it can serve as a moment of growth in faith and love.

By contemplating Christ's union with the Father even at the height of his sufferings on the cross (cf. Mark 15:34), Christians learn to share in the gaze of Jesus. Even death is illumined and can be experienced as the ultimate call to faith, the ultimate "Go forth from your land" (Gen 12:1), the ultimate "Come!" spoken by the Father, to whom we surrender ourselves in the confidence that he will be steadfast, present to us even in our final passage.

## An Icon of Mercy (15:39)[6]

Even the thief at the last hour let himself be drawn to the One who "had done nothing wrong" (cf. Luke 23:41). On seeing him pierced on the cross, those watching became aware of what they could never have recognized on their own had they not been moved by that love that they had never before known, that love that was poured out freely and abundantly! A distant and indifferent god can be ignored, but one cannot easily resist a God who is so close and, more than that, wounded out of love. The kindness, the beauty, the truth, the love, the goodness—see what we can offer this begging world, albeit in half-broken bowls.

However, it is not about bringing attention to oneself. This is a danger! The world is tired of lying charmers, and may I say, of "fashionable" priests or bishops. The people of God can "sense"—they have this gift from God—the people can "sense" and move away when they recognize narcissists, manipulators, defenders of their own causes, and preachers of vain crusades. Instead, try to move closer to God, who has already introduced himself before your arrival.

## Expectant Hope: Joseph of Arimathea (15:45)[7]

There is a vigilance that goes beyond mere attention: it is "expectant hope." We need to re-read the scriptures to see the righteous men, the pious women, and the faithful people of God who live this expectant hope: John the Baptist, who sent word by his disciples to ask Jesus if he was "the one who is to come" (Matt 11:3); or Joseph of Arimathea, who "waited" (Mark 15:43); or Simeon (Luke 2:25); or the faithful people to whom Anna, who "was waiting" (Luke 3:15), spoke (Luke 2:38).

We have to ask ourselves whether our vigilance includes this "hopeful waiting." Paul describes it in several ways: "my eager expectation and hope that I will not be put to shame in any way" (Phil 1:20); creation "waiting with eager longing for the revealing of the children of God" (Rom 8:19); and "while waiting for adoption as children, the redemption of our body... we wait for it with patience" (Rom 8:23–25).

This kind of hopeful expectation has the virtue of accelerating the coming of the kingdom of God, and therefore Saint Peter advises that while you are "waiting for and hastening the coming of the day of God ... strive to be found by him at peace, without spot or blemish" (2 Pet 3:12–14).

# 16
# Resurrection

## The Glory of the Cross (16:1)[1]

The Lord teaches us that those who must be perfected and healed are anointed: the dead are anointed (cf. Mark 16:1); the sick person is anointed (cf. Mark 6:13; Jas 5:14); wounds are anointed (cf. Luke 10:34); the penitent is anointed (cf. Matt 6:17). Anointing has a sense of reparation (Luke 7:38, 46; 10:34; John 11:2; 12:3). All this is valid for us: we are resurrected, healed, reformed, and renewed by the anointing of the Holy Spirit. Every yoke of slavery is destroyed because of the anointing (cf. Isa 10:27). The first anointed is the Lord (Luke 2:26; Acts 4:26; Luke 4:18; Acts 10:38). He was anointed with "the oil of gladness" (Heb 1:9).

Exultation calls us back to glory. To be anointed means to participate in the glory of Christ that is his cross. "Father, glorify your Son . . . Father, glorify your name" (cf. John 12:23, 28). Those who seek peace apart from the anointing do not seek the glory of God in the cross of Christ: "How can you believe when you accept glory from one another and do not seek the glory that comes from the one who alone is God?" (John 5:44).

## The Easter Vigil (16:1–7)[2]

At dawn, the women left their homes to go to the tomb. Earlier, they had bought aromatic oils to anoint Jesus's body. They had spent most of the night preparing everything in white and waiting until sunrise when there was enough light for them to go.

We too are sleepless tonight, not preparing to anoint the body of the Lord, but remembering the wonders of God in the history of humanity. Above all, we remember with great wonder the night he himself spent sleeplessly: "That was for the Lord a night of vigil, to bring them out of the land of Egypt. That same night is a vigil to be kept for the Lord by all the Israelites throughout their generations" (Exod 12:42).

This is the night when freedom is secured. And therefore, "This night is as clear as day."

Our life will continue with the light of what we celebrate during this vigil, and what happened to our fathers in the desert will also happen to us.

### *Fear paralyzes the heart, the hope*

We can be dominated by impatience, which leads us to prefer the occasional immediacy of idols (cf. Exod 32:1–6). In these moments it seems like the sun is hiding, the night returns, and our freedom enters an eclipse. When they came to the end of the night, the night of fear, Mary Magdalene, Mary the mother of James, and Salome went to the tomb. And then, even though the day had just begun, they "fled from the tomb" (Mark 16:8).

They ran away without saying anything to anyone. Fear made them forget what they had just heard: "You are looking for Jesus of Nazareth, who was crucified. He has been raised" (Mark 16:6). Fear silenced them so that they could not announce the news.

Fear *paralyzed their hearts* and they found safety in the feeling of failure instead of finding hope in the words of the one who said to them: "Go to Galilee, there you will see it." And this also happens to us: like them, we are afraid of hope and we prefer to take refuge within our limits, our smallness, and our sins; in doubts and denials that, right or wrong, we are committed to managing. They came in mourning, came to anoint a corpse and were amazed. . . . Basically, they were afraid of joy (cf. Luke 24:41).

## The First Day of the Week (16:2, 9)[3]

Through the Eucharist, that Easter morning is renewed—the passage of the Lord who willingly entered our world to make us partakers in his divine life. The Lord gathers us every Sunday as a family of God around the altar, to feed on the living Bread, to relive and celebrate events of the journey, to renew our strength, and to continue proclaiming that he is alive among us.

In every Sunday Mass, we experience our intimate belonging to the people of God, of which we became part through our baptism, and we recall that "first day of the week" (Mark 16:2, 9). In today's world, so often weighed down by secularism and consumerism, it seems that we are losing the ability to celebrate, to live as a family. The celebration is meant to endure in our hearts and give meaning and fullness for the rest of the week.

## Hope (16:9–15)[4]

On the evening of this first day of the week . . . a great disorientation reigned: many were sad, blocked by the fear of an attack by the same people who had killed Jesus, for fear that what had happened to the Lord would happen to them. They were afraid, says the Gospel. They kept the doors closed and spoke to each other: "What a pity, he died" . . . "No, look, some women went to the tomb this morning and they saw him" or "They saw some angels." And the comments were disconcerting: "They are out of their minds." "They had visions." "It's not true." And so they enveloped themselves in a climate of fear, frustration, and discouragement. That evening, the apostles became the first community of hopeless Christians, until the Lord appeared and with his presence cast out all the doubts, fears, and gossip and put everything in its place.

***Are we educating for hope?***

Many times a situation baffles us, problems overwhelm us and prevent us from seeing the horizon—as happened to these apostles who were crushed and overcome by the death of Christ. Educating in hope means making sure that people have horizons—open horizons, behind us and ahead of us.

## Proclaim the Good News (16:15, 20)[5]

Let us renew our confidence in preaching based on the conviction that it is God who seeks to reach out to others through the preacher, and that he displays his power through human words. Saint Paul speaks forcefully about the need to preach, since the Lord desires to reach other people by means of our words (cf. Rom 10:14–17). By his words our Lord won over the hearts of the people: they came from all parts to hear him (cf. Mark 1:45), they were amazed at his teachings (cf. Mark 6:2), and they sensed that he spoke to them as one with authority (cf. Mark 1:27). By their words the apostles, whom Christ established "to be with him and to be sent out to preach" (Mark 3:14), brought all nations to the bosom of the Church (cf. Mark 16:15, 20).

## Our Profession of Faith (16:15–16)[6]

Baptism is the "door" of faith and of Christian life. The risen Jesus left the apostles with this charge: "Go into all the world and preach the Gospel to the whole of creation. He who believes and is baptized will be saved" (Mark 16:15–16). The Church's mission is to evangelize and remit sins through the sacrament of baptism. But let us return to the words of the Creed and consider three elements: "I profess"; "one Baptism"; "for the remission of sins."

*"I profess."* What does this mean? It is a solemn term that indicates the great importance of the object, that is, of baptism. In fact, by pronouncing these words we affirm our true identity as children of God. Baptism is in a certain sense the identity card of the Christian, his or her birth certificate, and the act of his or her birth into the Church. All of you know the day on which you were born and you celebrate it as your birthday, don't you? We all celebrate our birthday. I ask you a question that I have already asked several times, but I'll ask it again: Who among you remembers the date of your baptism? . . . Today, when you go home, find out what day you were baptized. Look for it, because this is your second birthday. The first birthday is the day you came into life and the second birthday is the one on which you came into the Church.

At the same time, baptism is tied to our faith in the remission of sins. The sacrament of penance or confession is, in fact, like a "second baptism" that refers back always to the first to strengthen and renew it. In this sense, the day of our baptism is the point of departure for this most beautiful journey, a journey toward God that lasts a lifetime, a journey of conversion that is continually sustained by the sacrament of penance. Think about this: when we go to confess our weaknesses, our sins, we go to ask pardon of Jesus, but we also go to renew our baptism through his forgiveness. And this is beautiful. It is like celebrating the day of baptism at every confession. Therefore, confession is not a matter of sitting down in a torture chamber; rather, it is a celebration. Confession is for the baptized! It is meant to keep clean the white garment of our Christian dignity!

The second element: "*one baptism*." This expression refers to the words of Saint Paul: "one Lord, one faith, one baptism" (Eph 4:5). The word "baptism" literally means "immersion," and, in fact, this sacrament constitutes a true spiritual immersion in the death of Christ from which one rises with him like a new creation (cf. Rom 6:4). It is the washing of regeneration and of illumination: regeneration because it actuates that birth by water and the Spirit without which no one may enter the kingdom of Heaven (cf. John 3:5); illumination because through baptism the human person becomes filled with the grace of Christ, "the true light that enlightens every man" (John 1:9) and dispels the shadows of sin. That is why in the ceremony of baptism the parents are given a lit candle, to signify this illumination. Baptism illuminates us with the light of Jesus from within. In virtue of this gift, the baptized are called to become themselves "light"—the light of the faith they have received—for their brothers and sisters, especially for those who are in darkness and see no glimmer of light on the horizon of their lives.

We can ask ourselves: Is baptism, for me, a fact of the past, relegated to a date (that date that you are going to go look for today), or is it a living reality that pertains to my present, to every moment? Do I feel strong, with the strength that Christ gave me by his death and his resurrection? Or do I feel weak, without strength? Baptism gives strength, and it gives light. Do I feel enlightened with that light that comes from Christ? Am I a man or woman of light? Or am I a dark person without the light of Jesus? We need to take the grace of baptism, which is a gift, and become a light for all people!

Finally, a brief mention of the third element: "*for the remission of sins.*" In the sacrament of baptism all sins are remitted, original sin and all of our personal sins, as well as the suffering of sin. Through baptism, the door to a new life is opened, one that is not burdened by the weight of a negative past but rather already feels the beauty and the goodness of the kingdom of heaven. It is the powerful intervention of God's mercy in our lives, to save us. This saving intervention does not take away our human nature and its weakness—we are all weak and we are all sinners—and it does not take from us our responsibility to ask for forgiveness every time we err! I cannot be baptized many times, but I can go to confession and by doing so renew the grace of baptism. It is as though I were being baptized for a second time.

The Lord Jesus is very good and never tires of forgiving us. Even when the door that baptism opens to us in order to enter the church is a little closed, due to our weaknesses and our sins, confession reopens it, precisely because it is a second baptism that forgives us of everything and enables us to go forward with the light of the Lord. Let us go forward in this way, joyfully, because life should be lived with the joy of Jesus Christ, and this is a grace of the Lord.

# Bibliography


### *Vatican Documents*

The texts (homilies, meditations, speeches, Angelus, etc.) after the beginning of the pontificate are taken from: http://w2.vatican.va/content/vatican/en.html.

Congregation for the Doctrine of the Faith, Instruction *Libertatis Nuntius* (August 6, 1984), XI, 1: AAS 76 (1984).

Francis. *Amoris Laetitia*, Post-Synodal Apostolic Exhortation on Love in the Family (March 19, 2016).

Francis. *Evangelii Gaudium*, Apostolic Exhortation on the Proclamation of the Gospel in Today's World (November 24, 2013).

Francis. *Laudato Si'*, Encyclical Letter on Care for Our Common Home (May 24, 2015).

Francis. *Lumen Fidei*, Encyclical Letter on the Faith (June 29, 2013).

*Relatio Finalis*. Final Report of the Synod of Bishops to the Holy Father, Pope Francis, 2015.

*Relatio Synodi*. Report of the Third Extraordinary General Assembly of the Synod of Bishops, 2014.

### *Italian Sources*

Pope Francis. *Non fatevi rubare la speranza. La preghiera, il peccato, la filosofia e la politica pensati alla luce della speranza*. Milano: Oscar Mondadori; Città del Vaticano: LEV, 2014.

Jorge Mario Bergoglio–Pope Francis. *Agli educatori. Il pane della speranza. Non stancarti di seminare*. Città del Vaticano: LEV, 2014.

Jorge Mario Bergoglio–Pope Francis. *Aprite la mente al vostro cuore*. Milano: BUR–Rizzoli, 2014.

Jorge Mario Bergoglio–Pope Francis. *È l'amore che apre gli occhi*. Milano: Rizzoli, 2013.

Jorge Mario Bergoglio–Pope Francis. *Il desiderio allarga il cuore. Esercizi spirituali con il Papa*. Bologna: EMI, 2014.

Jorge Mario Bergoglio–Pope Francis. *In lui solo la speranza. Esercizi spirituali ai vescovi spagnoli* (January 15–22, 2006). Milano: Jaca Book; Città del Vaticano: LEV, 2013.

Jorge Mario Bergoglio–Pope Francis. *La misericordia è una carezza. Vivere il giubileo nella realtà di ogni giorno,* a cura di Antonio Spadaro. Milano: Rizzoli, 2015.

Jorge Mario Bergoglio. *Le parole di Papa Francesco, vols. 1-20,* Milano: Corriere della Sera, 2014–2015.

Jorge Mario Bergoglio–Pope Francis. *Nei tuoi occhi è la mia parola: Omelie e discorsi di Buenos Aires 1999–2013*. Milano: Rizzoli, 2016.

Jorge Mario Bergoglio–Pope Francis. *Nel cuore di ogni Padre. Alle radici della mia spiritualità*. Introduzione di Antonio Spadaro, SJ. Milano: Rizzoli, 2014.

Jorge Mario Bergoglio–Pope Francis. *Riflessioni di un pastore. Misericordia, Missione, Testimonianza, Vita.* Città del Vaticano: LEV, 2013.

Jorge Mario Bergoglio. *Solo l'amore ci può salvare*. Città del Vaticano: LEV, 2013.

# Notes

### *Introduction*

1. Antonio Spadaro, SJ, *"Percorrere cortili scorgendo praterie,"* Introduction in J. M. Bergoglio – Pope Francis, *Nel cuore di ogni Padre: Alle radici della mia spiritualità* (Milan: Rizzoli, 2014), 7.

### *1. The Beginning of the Public Life*

1. Pope Francis, "Communicating Hope and Trust in Our Time," Message for the Fifty-First World Communications Day, January 24, 2017.

2. Pope Francis, "Amid Memory and Hope," Morning Meditation, May 15, 2014.

3. Pope Francis, "The Gospel of Mercy," General Audience, April 6, 2016.

4. Pope Francis, "Feast of the Baptism of the Lord," Homily, January 11, 2015.

5. Pope Francis, Apostolic Exhortation, *Amoris Laetitia,* no. 71.

6. Pope Francis, Angelus, February 18, 2018.

7. Pope Francis, Angelus, January 25, 2015.

8. Pope Francis, "With the Gospel in Your Pocket," Morning Meditation, January 9, 2017.

9. Pope Francis, "Holy Mass on the Occasion of the 1050th Anniversary of the Baptism of Poland," On the Occasion of the Thirty-First World Youth Day, July 28, 2016.

10. Pope Francis, "Mercy and Conversion," Jubilee Audience, June 18, 2016.

11. Pope Francis, Address for the Meeting with the Bishops of Mexico during the Apostolic Journey to Mexico, February 13, 2016.

12. Pope Francis, "The Astonished Innkeeper," Morning Meditation, January 10, 2017.

13. Pope Francis, "Family and Illness," General Audience, June 10, 2015.

14. Pope Francis, Apostolic Exhortation, *Evangelii Gaudium*, no. 136.

15. Pope Francis, Angelus, February 4, 2018.

16. Pope Francis, Apostolic Exhortation, *Amoris Laetitia*, no. 21.

17. Pope Francis, "Victory and Defeat," Daily Meditation, February 14, 2016.

18. Pope Francis, Apostolic Exhortation, *Amoris Laetitia*, no. 289.

### *2. Healing and Preaching*

1. Pope Francis, General Audience, February 19, 2014.

2. Pope Francis, "A Seated Soul," Morning Meditation, January 13, 2017.

3. Pope Francis, Apostolic Exhortation, *Evangelii Gaudium*, no. 269.

4. Pope Francis, "New Wineskins," Morning Meditation, January 18, 2016.

5. Pope Francis, Address to Participants in the Third World Meeting of Popular Movements, November 5, 2016.

6. Cf. Homily at the First Congress of Evangelization of Culture, Buenos Aires, November 3, 2006.

### *3. The Teaching of Jesus*

1. Pope Francis, General Audience, June 10, 2015.

2. Pope Francis, "The Daily Struggle," Daily Meditation, January 19, 2017.

3. Pope Francis, "The Twelve Pillars," Morning Meditation, January 22, 2016.

4. Pope Francis, Apostolic Exhortation, *Evangelii Gaudium*, no. 36.

5. Pope Francis, "The Vessel of Mercy," A Spiritual Retreat on the Occasion of the Jubilee for Priests, Second Meditation, June 2, 2016.

6. Pope Francis, Address at the Meeting with Bishops Taking Part in the World Meeting of Families, St. Charles Borromeo Seminary, Philadelphia, September 27, 2015.

7. Pope Francis, "The Food of Jesus," Morning Meditation, January 27, 2015.

### *4. The Parables of Jesus*

1. Pope Francis, "Communicating Hope and Trust in Our Time," Message for the Fifty-First World Communications Day, January 24, 2017.

2. Pope Francis, "Fortitude," General Audience, May 14, 2014.

3. Pope Francis, "Without Measure," Morning Meditation, January 28, 2016.

4. Pope Francis, "Led by the Spirit for Mission," Message for the Fifty-Fourth World Day of Prayer for Vocations, November 27, 2016.

5. Pope Francis, Apostolic Exhortation, *Evangelii Gaudium*, no. 22.

6. Pope Francis, Angelus, June 17, 2018.

7. Pope Francis, Homily, Apostolic Journey to Georgia and Azerbaijan, October 1, 2016.

8. Pope Francis, Homily, Apostolic Journey to Poland on the Occasion of the Thirty-First World Youth Day; Mass for the 105th Anniversary of the Baptism of Poland, July 28, 2016.

### *5. The Miracles of Jesus*

1. Pope Francis, "Jesus Looks at Each of Us," Morning Meditation, January 31, 2017.

2. Pope Francis, "The Gospel in Hand," Morning Meditation, February 3, 2015.

3. Pope Francis, "When God Cries," Morning Meditation, February 4, 2014.

4. Pope Francis, Angelus, June 28, 2015.

5. Pope Francis, "The Sweet Smell of Christ and the Light of His Mercy," Spiritual Retreat on the Occasion of the Jubilee for Priests, Third Meditation, June 2, 2016.

6. Pope Francis, Apostolic Exhortation, *Amoris Laetitia,* no. 100.

7. Pope Francis, "The Sweet Smell of Christ and the Light of His Mercy," Spiritual Retreat on the Occasion of the Jubilee for Priests, Third Meditation, June 2, 2016.

### *6. The Ministry of Jesus*

1. Pope Francis, Apostolic Exhortation, *Amoris Laetitia,* no. 182.

2. Pope Francis, Encyclical, *Laudato Si',* no. 98.

3. Pope Francis, "I Will Cure You," Morning Meditation, February 5, 2015.

4. Pope Francis, Homily, Holy Mass at Campo Grande, Paraguay, July 12, 2015.

5. Pope Francis, "The Great One's Darkest Hour," Morning Meditation, February 6, 2015.

6. Pope Francis, "Return to the First Galilee," Morning Meditation, February 7, 2014.

7. Pope Francis, Address at the Meeting with the Bishops of Mexico, February 13, 2016.

8. Pope Francis, Angelus, July 19, 2015.

9. Pope Francis, "Feed the Hungry, Give Drink to the Thirsty," General Audience, October 19, 2016.

10. Pope Francis, "Overcome Indifference and Win Peace," Fifty-Fourth World Day of Peace, January 1, 2016.

11. Pope Francis, "May the Lord Change the Hearts of the Cruel," Morning Meditation, January 8, 2015.

12. Pope Francis, Apostolic Exhortation, *Evangelii Gaudium,* no. 49.

13. Pope Francis, Apostolic Exhortation, *Evangelii Gaudium,* no. 188.

14. Congregation for the Doctrine of the Faith, Instruction *Libertatis Nuntius* (August 6, 1984), XI, 1: AAS 76 (1984), 903.

15. Pope Francis, "Hardened Hearts," Morning Meditation, January 9, 2015.

16. Pope Francis, "Working with God," Morning Meditation, February 9, 2015.

### *7. Clean and Unclean*

1. Pope Francis, "Two Identity Cards," Morning Meditation, February 10, 2015.

2. Pope Francis, Angelus, September 2, 2018.

3. Pope Francis, Apostolic Exhortation, *Amoris Laetitia*, nos. 188–190.

4. Pope Francis, Message for the Thirtieth World Youth Day, January 31, 2015.

5. Pope Francis, Address to Participants in the Plenary Assembly of the Pontifical Academy for Life, March 3, 2016.

6. Pope Francis, Message for the Celebration of the Fiftieth World Day of Peace, January 1, 2017.

7. Saint Francis, "The Legend of the Three Companions," *Franciscan Sources*, No. 1469.

8. Pope Francis, "The King and the Woman," Morning Meditation, February 13, 2014.

9. Pope Francis, Angelus, September 6, 2015.

### *8. The Mission and the Cross*

1. Pope Francis, Homily for the Apostolic Journey to Ecuador, Bolivia, and Paraguay, Christ the Redeemer Square, Bolivia, July 9, 2015.

2. Pope Francis, "Holy Patience," Morning Meditation, February 17, 2014.

3. Pope Francis, "Resist Temptation," Morning Meditation, February 18, 2014.

4. Pope Francis, "As Martyrs," Morning Meditation, February 17, 2015.

5. Pope Francis, "But Who Do You Say That I Am?" Morning Meditation, February 20, 2014.

6. Pope Francis, General Audience, March 27, 2013.

### *9. Glory and the Cross*

1. Pope Francis, Angelus, March 1, 2015.
2. Pope Francis, "Returning Home," Morning Meditation, February 24, 2014.
3. Pope Francis, "The Desire to Climb," Morning Meditation, May 17, 2016.
4. Pope Francis, "Worldly Temptations," Morning Meditation, February 21, 2017.
5. Pope Francis, Homily, Apostolic Journey to Cuba, to the United States of America, and Visit to the United Nations Headquarters, Havana, Cuba, September 20, 2015.
6. Pope Francis, Address to His Grace Justin Welby, Archbishop of Canterbury and His Entourage, June 16, 2014.
7. Pope Francis, Message for the World Day of Migrants and Refugees, January 15, 2017.
8. Pope Francis, Address at the Meeting with the Children of the "Centro Bethania" and the Representatives from Other Charitable Centers of Albania, Bethany, Tirana, September 21, 2014.
9. Pope Francis, "Do Not Delay Conversion," Morning Meditation, February 23, 2017.
10. Pope Francis, "The Scandal of Inconsistency," Morning Meditation, February 27, 2014.

### *10. Discipleship*

1. Pope Francis, Apostolic Exhortation, *Amoris Laetitia*, no. 63.
2. *Relatio Synodi*, Report of the III Extraordinary General Assembly of the Synod of Bishops, 2014, 16.
3. Pope Francis, "Justice and Mercy," Morning Meditation, February 24, 2017.
4. Pope Francis, "God Is Not an Equation," Morning Meditation, May 20, 2016.
5. Pope Francis, Apostolic Exhortation, *Amoris Laetitia*, no. 71.
6. *Relatio Finalis*, Final Report of the Synod of Bishops to the Holy Father, Pope Francis, 2015, 38.

7. Pope Francis, General Audience, March 18, 2015.

8. Pope Francis, "The Food of Jesus," Morning Meditation, January 27, 2015.

9. Pope Francis, Message for the Thirtieth World Youth Day 2015, January 31, 2015.

10. Pope Francis, "Beguiled by the Serpent," Morning Meditation, May 25, 2015.

11. Pope Francis, "Ode to Joy," Morning Meditation, May 23, 2016.

12. Pope Francis, Angelus, October 11, 2015.

13. Pope Francis, Apostolic Exhortation, *Amoris Laetitia*, no. 323.

14. *Relatio Finalis* (2015), no. 88.

15. Pope Francis, Apostolic Exhortation, *Evangelii Gaudium*, no. 269.

16. Pope Francis, "Our Wage from Jesus," Morning Meditation, May 26, 2015.

17. Pope Francis, "Everything and Nothing," Morning Meditation, February 28, 2017.

18. Pope Francis, Homily, Ordinary Public Consistory for the Creation of New Cardinals, February 22, 2014.

19. Pope Francis, Angelus, October 21, 2018.

20. Pope Francis, Homily, Jubilee of Deacons, May 29, 2016.

21. Pope Francis, Homily, Closing of the Ordinary General Assembly of the Synod of Bishops, October 25, 2015.

22. Pope Francis, "What Kind of Christian Are We?" Morning Meditation, May 28, 2015.

23. Pope Francis, Jubilee Audience, May 14, 2016.

### *11. Jerusalem*

1. Pope Francis, Homily, Palm Sunday, Twenty-Eighth World Youth Day, March 24, 2013.

2. Pope Francis, "Three Lifestyles," Morning Meditation, May 29, 2015.

3. Pope Francis, "Authority Is Not in Commanding but in Consistent Witness," Morning Meditation, January 14, 2020.

### *12. Temple of Jerusalem*

1. Pope Francis, Jubilee Audience, June 18, 2016.

2. Pope Francis, "Salvation Is Drawn from Rejection," Morning Meditation, June 1, 2015.

3. Pope Francis, "The Caged Spirit," Morning Meditation, May 30, 2016.

4. Pope Francis, "The Hypocrite Is Always a Flatterer," Morning Meditation, June 6, 2017.

5. Pope Francis, Angelus, November 4, 2018.

6. Pope Francis, Angelus, November 8, 2015.

7. Pope Francis, Angelus, November 11, 2018.

### *13. Being Prepared*

1. J. M. Bergoglio – Pope Francis, "Homily for the Mass for the Opening of the Plenary Assembly of the Bishops Conference, Argentina, Pilar, April 23, 2007," in *È l'amore che apre gli occhi* (Milano: Rizzoli, 2013), 157–81.

2. Pope Francis, Jubilee Audience, June 18, 2016.

3. Pope Francis, Angelus, December 3, 2017.

### *14. The Passion*

1. J. M. Bergoglio – Pope Francis, "Homily for the Feast of the Presentation of the Lord, Buenos Aires, February 2, 2008," in *Solo l'amore ci può salvare* (Vatican City: LEV, 2013).

2. Pope Francis, Homily for the Solemnity of the Most Holy Body and Blood of Christ, June 3, 2018.

3. Pope Francis, Angelus, June 7, 2015.

4 . J. M. Bergoglio – Pope Francis, *"L'esilio della carne: la preghiera della carne in esilio,"* in *Aprite la mente al vostro cuore* (Milan: BUR–Rizzoli, 2014), 199–203; Pope Francis, *Non fatevi rubare la speranza* (Milan: Oscar Mondadori / Vatican City: LEV, 2014), 15–19.

5. J. M. Bergoglio – Pope Francis, *"Il mistero dell'avvicinamento a*

*Dio,"* in *Aprite la mente al vostro cuore,* 222–229; Pope Francis, *Non fatevi rubare la speranza,* 225–231.

6. J. M. Bergoglio – Pope Francis, *"Il Signore che ci riprende e perdona,"* in *In lui solo la speranza. Esercizi spirituali ai vescovi spagnoli* (January 15–22, 2006) (Milan: Jaca Book / Vatican City: LEV, 2013); J. M. Bergoglio–Pope Francis, *Nel cuore di ogni Padre* (Vatican City: LEV, 2014), 238–244.

### *15. Crucifixion and Burial*

1. J. M. Bergoglio, *"Il silenzio,"* in *Natale* (*Le parole di papa Francesco,* 1) (Milan: Corriere della Sera, 2014), 67–83.

2. Pope Francis, *"L'accanimento,"* in *Non fatevi rubare la speranza. La preghiera, il peccato, la filosofia e la politica pensati alla luce della speranza,* (Milan: Mondadori / Vatican City: LEV, 2014), 103–105.

3. J. M. Bergoglio – Pope Francis, *"I nostri padri sono stati tentati,"* in *Nel cuore di ogni Padre. Alle radici della mia spiritualità, Introduzione di Antonio Spadaro S.J.* (Milan: Rizzoli, 2014), 170–175.

4. Pope Francis, Angelus, Feast of Christ the King, November 22, 2015.

5. Pope Francis, Encyclical, *Lumen Fidei,* no. 56.

6. Pope Francis, Address to the Newly Appointed Bishops participating in the Formative Courses Organized by the Congregations for Bishops and for Oriental Churches, September 16, 2016.

7. J. M. Bergoglio – Pope Francis, *"Aspettando l'epifania,"* in *Aprite la mente al vostro cuore,* 104–107; Pope Francis, *Non fatevi rubare la speranza,* 54–57.

### *16. Resurrection*

1. J. M. Bergoglio – Pope Francis, *"Il silenzio,"* in *Natale* (*Le parole di papa Francesco,* 1) (Milan: Corriere della Sera, 2014), 67–83.

2. J. M. Bergoglio – Pope Francis, *"Non aver paura,"* in *Riflessioni di un pastore. Misericordia, Missione, Testimonianza, Vita* (Vatican City: LEV, 2013); see "Omelia, Vigilia di Pasqua, Buenos Aires, 7 aprile

2012"; J. M. Bergoglio – Pope Francis, "*Non abbiate paura,*" in *Agli educatori. Il pane della speranza. Non stancarti di seminare* (Vatican City: LEV, 2014), 67–69.

3. J. M. Bergoglio – Pope Francis, "*Lettera ai catechisti,* Buenos Aires, agosto 2001," in *Nei tuoi occhi è la mia parola: Omelie e discorsi di Buenos Aires 1999–2013,* (Milan: Rizzoli, 2016), 120–25.

4. J. M. Bergoglio – Pope Francis, "Omelia, Messa per l'educazione, Buenos Aires, 14 aprile 2010," in *Nei tuoi occhi è la mia parola,* 768–71.

5. Pope Francis, Apostolic Exhortation, *Evangelii Gaudium,* no. 136.

6. Pope Francis, General Audience, November 13, 2013.

Made in the USA
Monee, IL
02 November 2020